MONKSTOWN

A VICTORIAN VILLAGE

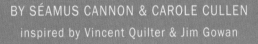

BY SÉAMUS CANNON & CAROLE CULLEN

inspired by Vincent Quilter & Jim Gowan

MONKSTOWN

A VICTORIAN VILLAGE

BY SÉAMUS CANNON & CAROLE CULLEN
inspired by Vincent Quilter & Jim Gowan

Blackrock Education Centre
Ionad Oideachais na Carraige Duibhe

Blackrock Education Centre 2014

ISBN 978-0-9564074-9-8

Published by
Blackrock Education Centre, Kill Avenue, Dún Laoghaire, Co. Dublin, Ireland
Tel: (+353 1)236 5000
Email: becbooks@blackrockec.ie / Web: www.becpublishing.com

First published 2014

Authors
Séamus Cannon
Carole Cullen

Editorial Committee
Séamus Cannon, Carole Cullen, Carrie Fonseca, Étain Murphy, Colin Scudds and Noel Tierney

Editor
Claire Rourke

Graphic Design and Formatting
Eliane Pearce
www.elianepearce.com

Cover Design
Eliane Pearce
www.elianepearce.com

Contents

Acknowledgements

Many people have contributed to the creation of this book. Fr. Vincent Quilter and Dr. Jim Gowan prepared a typescript in 1991 with a view to publication and this has been the primary inspiration for this work. We owe them a great debt of gratitude and we also thank the Quilter and Gowan families for their encouragement and support. We would also like to particularly acknowledge our reliance on the original works by Étain Murphy (*A Glorious Extravaganza*) and Peter Pearson (*From the Mountains to the Sea*). The Dún Laoghaire Borough Historical Society and the Blackrock Society were supportive and nominated representatives to our editorial board to make it a truly community effort.

The Editorial Board of Étain Murphy, Colin Scudds (Dún Laoghaire Borough Historical Society) and Noel Tierney (Blackrock Society) were always encouraging and helpful in critiquing drafts of the text and in sourcing information; Emlyn Cullen's thesis on Monkstown Castle was most helpful; several friends read portions of the text and offered advice and constructive criticism: Peter Pearson, Bill Hastings and Rob Goodbody; others also generously shared their expertise: Tom Conlon, Cormac Lowth, Tony Dunne and Julian Deale; Frank Hegarty contributed the biographical note on Admiral Beechey.

Many residents and shopkeepers were also most forthcoming in sharing their stories and their sources. A special word of thanks therefore to Thelma and David Hewett, Roberts Family, John White, Nuala Kavanagh, Ruth Grant, Maria Cole, Hannah Cameron, the Dempsey Family, Maurice Keegan, Caroline Mullan and Peter Derbyshire. We would also like to thank the church leaders in our community Fr. Michael Coady, the Rev. Canon Patrick Lawrence and Mr. Neville Keary for their leadership in establishing MC3, the community of Christian churches in Monkstown.

Dún Laoghaire County Council is to be commended for the manner in which it promotes awareness of our local heritage through enlightened planning and through the work of the Heritage Office. We gratefully acknowledge the grant we received towards publication, and the assistance and encouragement we were afforded by Heritage Officer, Tim Carey.

The staff of the National Library of Ireland, the Royal Irish Academy and the Ordnance Survey of Ireland have been most helpful and co-operative.

We would like to thank the management and staff of Blackrock Education Centre for its publishing expertise and in particular Pat Seaver (Director) and Carrie Fonseca (Publishing Manager). Designer Eliane Pearce has demonstrated skill, imagination and patience in equal measure and Claire Rourke has been a very thorough editor.

Any errors or omissions are the responsibility of the authors.

Séamus Cannon and Carole Cullen

Foreword

The title, *Monkstown: A Victorian Village,* says it all. Monkstown, today, retains its original scale and atmosphere much as its nineteenth century builders left it.

This affectionate and evocative celebration of the social and architectural heritage of Monkstown was inspired by the original research of two Monkstown residents, Fr. Vincent Quilter PP and Dr. Jim Gowan, who intended to publish their work under the title *Monkstown: The Story of an Old Dublin Community.* As it happened, publication at that time was too costly and so the manuscript was left aside. After Fr. Quilter's death, the only copy of the transcript was passed on to Carole Cullen, who had taken black and white photographs to illustrate the original text.

Several years later, Carole contacted Séamus Cannon and together they decided to explore its possible publication. They then consulted with the Gowan and Quilter families. Neither family knew of the existence of the manuscript and both were supportive of the initiative.

An editorial committee was formed comprising local historian Étain Murphy, Colin Scudds (Dún Laoghaire Borough Historical Society), Noel Tierney (Blackrock Society) as well as the authors, both of whom are local residents. Blackrock Education Centre agreed to publish the work and Carrie Fonseca, head of the publishing division in the Centre, joined the editorial committee. Designer, Eliane Pearce, also a local resident, completed the team.

Following a close study of the manuscript, it was decided that the document could no longer be published in its original form since that concept had been overtaken by subsequent publications. It was concluded that an entire rewrite was required and this gave the opportunity to commission new colour photographs. Séamus Cannon undertook the rewriting and Carole Cullen the illustration.

An application to Dún Laoghaire Rathdown Heritage Office for grant aid was successful. Contributions were also made by the Quilter family, Dún Laoghaire Borough Historical Society, Blackrock Society, and many individuals and businesses who responded to an invitation to 'crowd-fund' the production. Without their generosity we would not have this fine account of our shared history and heritage. Ní neart go cur le chéile.

Blackrock Education Centre has a proud record of promoting local studies in schools and in the community through teacher training courses and the creation of learning materials for students. Previous publications include *The Book of Dún Laoghaire* and *The Book of Bray,* a series of walks in the area entitled *The Dún Laoghaire Way,* a video *The Shaping of Dún Laoghaire* and e-learning project, *Trails, which was a* winner of a National Digital Media Award.

Blackrock Education Centre is honoured to publish *Monkstown: A Victorian Village* and so play its part in promoting community in our area. We are proud to work in association with the community partners involved – Dún Laoghaire Borough Historical Society, Blackrock Society and Dún Laoghaire Rathdown County Council.

Congratulations to Carole and Séamus on bringing together an artist's eye and a historian's words to create a wonderful record of Monkstown's rich and varied past. This splendid book will inform, inspire and no doubt bring pleasure and pride to the residents of Monkstown for generations to come.

Cora Quinn
Chairperson, Blackrock Education Centre

Introduction

Since Fr. Vincent Quilter and Dr. Jim Gowan wrote *Monkstown: The Story of an Old South Dublin Community* in 1990, a number of new publications have transformed our understanding of the history of our area. Two in particular stand out: *From the Mountains to the Sea* by Peter Pearson and *A Glorious Extravaganza* by Étain Murphy. In addition to these, there have been many articles published by the Dún Laoghaire Borough Historical Society and the Blackrock Society and by other scholarly journals. The internet of course greatly facilitates research in a way that had not been available to Fr. Quilter and Dr. Jim Gowan.

These new sources have enabled us to rewrite the text entirely and to illustrate it in full colour. In doing so, we have endeavoured to keep to the spirit that inspired the original authors, to write a book that tells the story of Monkstown for the general reader. While neither Fr. Quilter nor Dr. Gowan were natives of Monkstown, they developed a great affection for the area and the people which comes across in what they wrote. They were both avid local historians and the manuscript they prepared was comprehensive and thorough. While we have rewritten the text, their influence is evident in the presentation of the material in three sections: A History of Monstown; the Buildings of Monkstown and Notable Residents. There was also a certain looseness in determining the boundaries of Monkstown and this remains.

It may well be that this book had its genesis in the commitment and foresight of those volunteers who undertook the restoration of the Old Monkstown Graveyard in 1984, a project in which Fr. Quilter and the Dún Laoghaire Historical Society were intimately involved. Jim Gowan was, of course, also a leading light in the society. Other statutory and voluntary groups were involved including An Taisce and AnCO, the predecessor of FÁS in a very significant community project that heightened awareness of Monkstown's cultural heritage. Teacher Valerie Smyth instigated this project with class M2 from Dún Laoghaire Community College (now DFEI).

Today's Monkstown is largely a creation of the nineteenth century, when the development of a commuter railway and the harbour at Dún Laoghaire (then Kingstown) made it an attractive residential area. It became a suburb of substantial houses occupied by successful business people and wealthy professionals. Graceful terraces and avenues complement the large detached houses to create a pleasing unified built environment. The scale, intimacy and architectural detail of the village shops, clustered beside the churches, also contribute to the atmosphere of another age.

Behind this Victorian facade lies an older Monkstown, which took its name from the Cistercian monks of Monkstown Castle, built in the thirteenth century to protect the extensive monastic lands from attack by the displaced native Irish. A local tradition suggests an even older monastic settlement in the late eighth century, in the grounds of Carrickbrennan Graveyard. Monkstown has a rich and varied history.

Monkstown residents have made major contributions to society at home and abroad. Two major international missionary movements focusing on health care originated in Monkstown, The Leprosy Mission and the Medical Missionaries of Mary; distinguished humanitarians from Monkstown campaigned vigorously for improvements in the conditions of the poor and made a great contribution to famine relief; a fascinating group of scientists, several of them astronomers, lived in Monkstown. This third chapter of the book overwhelmingly features men, reflecting the fact that very few women worked outside the home, or had access to further education. For that reason, the women featured here can be regarded as particularly outstanding. One cannot imagine a similarly disproportionate representation in the twentieth century.

Today, Monkstown has been transformed with the development of housing estates and apartment blocks, but it has retained its Victorian atmosphere in the integrity of its architecture and in the intimate scale of its shops. It has also retained a vigorous commitment to social

justice evident in twentieth century initiatives like The Samaritans, the Irish branch of which originated in Monkstown and the international aid agency, Goal.

It is our hope that this book will contribute to a deepening of the sense of community in Monkstown, and to a greater appreciation of its rich heritage.

Séamus Cannon and *Carole Cullen*

BATHING PLACE SEAPOINT 1900s

Biographical Notes

Dr. Jim Gowan was born in 1925, a native of Skerries, Co. Dublin. He was educated in UCD and later lectured in Organic Chemistry in University College London, and in UCD. He was an avid local historian and was a founder member of the Dún Laoghaire Borough Historical Society. He presented the society's first lecture entitled 'An Evening of Local History' in the Royal Marine Hotel on the 20 June 1978. So popular was it that the lecture was repeated a short time later. He lectured regularly to the society and took a particular interest in the history of Monkstown. He lived in Castle Park where he was highly regarded as a gardener by his neighbours. Jim Gowan died in 2002.

Fr. Vincent Quilter was born in 1932 in Co. Kerry, and attended St Brendan's College in Killarney. He studied for the priesthood in Clonliffe College. He was appointed curate in Monkstown parish in 1977 and took a great interest in everything to do with its history. He joined in enthusiastically with the celebrations of the bicentenary of Monkstown Church of Ireland on 16 September 1989. It was with some sadness that he left Monkstown to take up duties first in Celbridge and finally in Whitehall parish, where he died in 1998.

Dr. Séamus Cannon is an educationalist with a love of local history. He has lectured to the Blackrock Society and to Dún Laoghaire Borough Historical Society, as well as in his native Donegal. He edited *The Book of Dún Laoghaire* and *The Book of Bray,* and has produced a range of resources in digital media. He is a former Director of Blackrock Education Centre. Séamus lives in Castle Park and is married to Bronagh O'Hanlon.

Carole Cullen is a local artist and photographer. Carole collaborated with Fr. Quilter in his early research and retained the only copy of the typescript which provided the inspiration for this publication. She teaches both art and photography. Carole lives on Monkstown Road. and is married to Leo Cullen.

ROCQUES MAP 1756

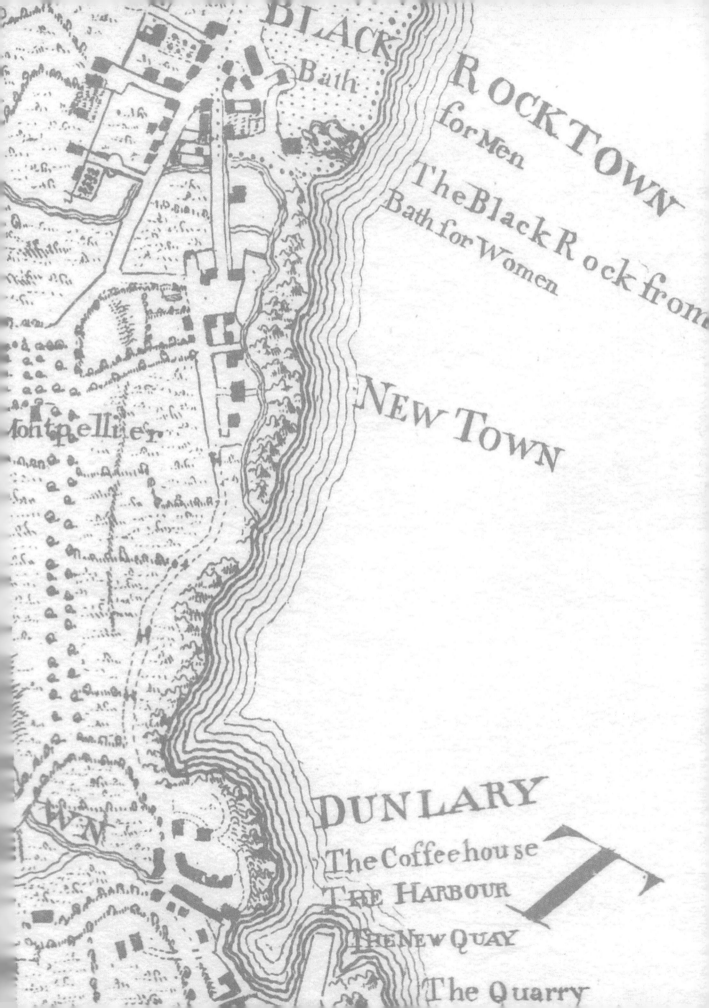

BLACK

ROCK TOWN

Bath

for Men

The Black Rock from

Bath for Women

Montpellier

NEW TOWN

DUN LARY

The Coffeehouse

THE HARBOUR

The New Quay

The Quarry

CHAPTER 1

The History of Monkstown

Early History

What's in a Name?

Monkstown takes its name from the monks of St Mary's Abbey in Dublin, who were granted extensive lands in the area during the first half of the twelfth century. Originally a Benedictine monastery on the north side of the Liffey (it gave its name to Abbey Street and Mary Street in Dublin), St Mary's submitted to Cistercian rule in 1147 during a period of reform in the Irish Church.

The name Monkstown is first mentioned in 1540 following the dissolution of the monasteries during the English Reformation in the reign of Henry VIII. The reference is to *Caribrynan alias Monketown*, which refers to a yet earlier name we know today as Carrickbrennan. *Karibrenan* is first mentioned in 1171, and there is some speculation as to its origin. It derives from the Irish 'carraig Bhraonáin' and has been associated by some authors with St Brendan, but is more likely a personal name meaning the 'rock of Braonáin'. As can be seen in some old street signs, Carraig Bhraonáin has, at times, been regarded as the Irish-language name for Monkstown.

Early Traditions

There is a tradition that an earlier monastery was established in the place where the old Monkstown graveyard now stands. The story goes that, in 798, the monastery founded by St Mochanna on Inispatrick off the coast of Skerries, was plundered by the Vikings and that the monks fled by currach, carrying the relics of their founder, and came ashore at the creek estuary at Dún Laoghaire. This was the only inlet on the south side of the bay. Having landed, they proceeded up the course of the stream and established their monastery. This story gives us a starting date for Monkstown, and the 1,200 anniversary of Monkstown was celebrated in a Village Day in 1998. However, there is no sure historical basis for this date and no archaeological remains of an earlier settlement have been found.

THE CHURCH RUIN IN CARRICKBRENNAN GRAVEYARD

The Cistercians in Monkstown

From 1147 until the Reformation, the history of Monkstown was integrated into the history of St Mary's Abbey in Dublin. The Cistercian monks were very skilled in agriculture and fishing and were great builders in stone. The monks cultivated the land and had fishing rights in Bullock. Carrickbrennan was constituted a manor (i.e a feudal domain) in the thirteenth century. Monkstown Castle and Bullock castle were built for protection from the local displaced Irish, principally the O'Byrnes and O'Tooles. The Cistercians were favoured by the Norman conquerors, not least because they were a French order and represented the reforming church which had been a critical justification of the Norman invasion. With the further grant of lands near modern Blackrock in 1220, the lands of the manor extended from near Dalkey to the Glaslower, or lepers' stream on the outskirts of Blackrock. This stream enters the sea at Maretimo.

Monkstown Castle

Before the Norman conquest, the Irish monks had the protection of the local Irish lord, Mac Giollamacholmóg but, after the conquest of Ireland, the monks were replaced by monks from the great Cistercian monastery of Buildwas in Shropshire, who were regarded as fair game by the native Irish.

Monkstown Castle was the most distinctive landmark of ancient Monkstown and local history has been bound up with the castle for many hundreds of years.

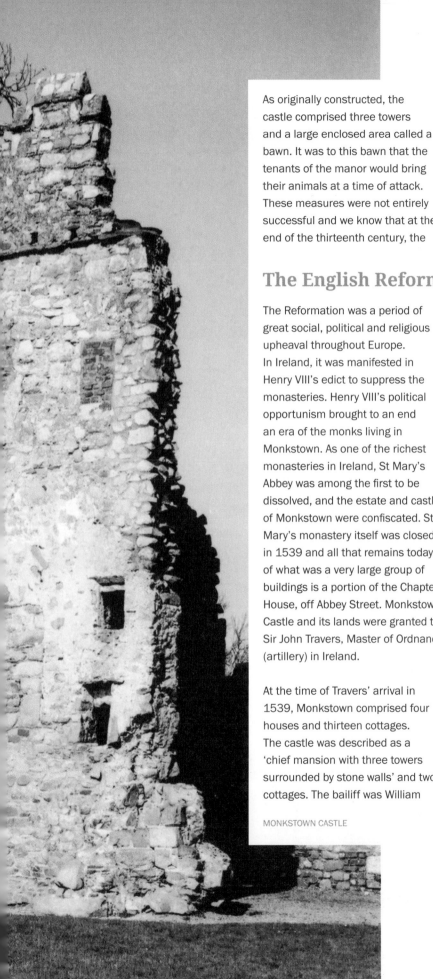

As originally constructed, the castle comprised three towers and a large enclosed area called a bawn. It was to this bawn that the tenants of the manor would bring their animals at a time of attack. These measures were not entirely successful and we know that at the end of the thirteenth century, the lands of Carrickbrennan, which had been made a manor earlier in the century, were so reduced as to be insufficient to support a chaplain. A smaller castle was built at Newtown, on the coast and this settlement became Newtown-on-the-Strand, the forerunner of modern-day Blackrock.

The English Reformation in Monkstown

The Reformation was a period of great social, political and religious upheaval throughout Europe. In Ireland, it was manifested in Henry VIII's edict to suppress the monasteries. Henry VIII's political opportunism brought to an end an era of the monks living in Monkstown. As one of the richest monasteries in Ireland, St Mary's Abbey was among the first to be dissolved, and the estate and castle of Monkstown were confiscated. St Mary's monastery itself was closed in 1539 and all that remains today of what was a very large group of buildings is a portion of the Chapter House, off Abbey Street. Monkstown Castle and its lands were granted to Sir John Travers, Master of Ordnance (artillery) in Ireland.

At the time of Travers' arrival in 1539, Monkstown comprised four houses and thirteen cottages. The castle was described as a 'chief mansion with three towers surrounded by stone walls' and two cottages. The bailiff was William

MONKSTOWN CASTLE

Kelly and the names of residents were: John Gavan, James McShane, John O'Moran, William Fullam, Walter Coleman, John Long, Denis O'Finn, Thomas McMyles, Patrick Frynde, Patrick Bayley, David Vengill, James Cogan, John and William Lacy, John Taylor, Patrick Gygin, Hugh White and Simon Brown.

With the arrival of Travers, Monkstown's association with the Cistercians came to an end. Sir John was engaged in extensive military campaigning with Lord Grey and Sir Anthony St Leger throughout Ireland and claimed that, with 2,000 men, he could go anywhere in Ireland. He was also highly regarded for his political views and was appointed to the Lord Deputy's Council. He was described as 'a native of Ireland' and may have been an Irish speaker. Travers retired to Monkstown Castle in 1557 and died there in 1562. He is buried in Carrickbrennan Graveyard. On his death, the castle passed to his grand-daughter, Mary.

The Cheevers of Monkstown

Mary Travers married James Eustace, Viscount Baltinglass, a prominent Catholic and an opponent of the English Reformation. The Catholic religion was still suppressed and Protestantism was seen by a large majority of the population as a religion imposed by an imported clergy, speaking a foreign tongue. Two of James Eustace's brothers were executed and he himself was imprisoned for a time. He threw in his lot with the Earl of Desmond's revolt in Kerry but, when this was violently suppressed, he fled to Spain where he died in 1585.

Mary remarried and lived until 1610. She had no male heir and on her death, the estate fell to her nephew, Henry Cheevers of Macetown, County Meath, also a Catholic. Henry Cheevers maintained a mass-house locally and supported a Catholic priest named Fr Turlough O'Reilly. Henry Cheevers is also buried in Carrickbrennan Graveyard. On his death, he was succeeded by his son, Walter.

Walter Cheevers had a considerably more turbulent stay than his father. It was a time of heightened religious tension in England, leading to the Civil War which culminated in the dethronement and execution of King Charles I in 1649. The monarchy was abolished and parliament enacted punitive legislation against Catholics. The English Civil War also had its echoes in Ireland when a violent revolt, which had begun in Ulster in 1641, spread throughout the country. For some years, Kilkenny was the capital of Ireland and the pope became very involved in Irish affairs, causing great alarm to the authorities. In 1649, Cromwell took command of the army in Ireland and brutally suppressed the rebellion. This was followed by the Cromwellian Plantation, in which Catholics were dispossessed and their lands granted to loyal Protestants.

CHEVERS OF IRELAND

'To Hell or to Connaught'

In the Cromwellian Plantation, Monkstown was granted to Lieutenant-General Edmund Ludlow, second in command of Cromwell's forces in Ireland. Walter Cheevers was given the choice of going 'to Hell or to Connaught' – Hell, the loss of his eternal reward if he renounced his faith, or exile in Connaught if he refused. Cheevers chose Connaught and, on 16 December 1653, he was ordered to Connaught with his family and servants. He was required to supply the English authorities with a statement of his goods and a description of all who were to accompany him. This document has survived and reads as follows:

Walter Cheevers, of sanguine complexion, brown haire, and indifferent statue [stature]; his wife Alison Netterville, otherwise Cheevers, with five children, the eldest not above seven years old; four women servants and seven menservants; viz Daniel Barry, tall statue, red beard, bald pate; Thady Cullen, of small statue, brown haire on his face; Morgan Cullen, of small statue, blind of one eye, with black haire; Philip Birne, aged about 40 years, black haire, low statue; William Birne, tall statue, aged 35 years; Patrick Corbally, aged 40 years, red haire, middle statue. The said Walter doth manure twenty colpe of corn and hath twenty cows, sixty sheep, thirty hoggs, two ploughs of garrans [horses].

The tenants willing to remove with him are: Arthur Birne, of little statue, brown haire, aged about 30 years; Dudley Birne, middle statue, brown haire, aged about twenty-five years; which tenants have a plough of garrans, twelve cows, forty sheep; Martin Maguire, tall of statue and red haire, aged 30 years, hath six cows, four garrans, twenty sheep; Thos. Eustace, lowe statue, brown haire, twenty-five years, hath ten cows, forty sheep, a plough of garrans and ten hoggs. The substance whereof we conceive to be true. In witness, whereof we have hereunto set our hands and seals, the 19th Day of December 1653.

We can imagine the hardship the family and their retainers endured on that Christmas journey.

General Ludlow was responsible for many improvements to Monkstown Castle during his seven years there, including landscaping the gardens and the establishment of a yew walk, the remnants of which can still be seen. At the restoration of the monarchy in 1660, after the death of Cromwell, Ludlow, who had signed the king's death warrant, felt that his own life was in danger (several regicides were executed) and he retired to Berne in Switzerland. There, he wrote his memoirs which include many references to Monkstown. He died in 1692.

OPPOSITE PAGE, **TOP** CHEEVERS FAMILY COAT OF ARMS **BOTTOM** *MONKSTOWN CASTLE* BY GABRIEL BERANGER 1766 **THIS PAGE** MONKSTOWN CASTLE BY GEORGE PETRIE, 1819

Cheevers' Family Return

The Cheevers family returned to Monkstown in 1660 at the start of Charles II's reign. Walter Cheevers did not remain long at Monkstown however, and soon retired to his castle at Newtown-on-the-Strand, on the northern boundary of his estate, adjacent to modern Blackrock. His daughter married a member of the Byrne family of Cabinteely, hence the early name 'Newtown Castlebyrne' for modern-day Blackrock.

The Cheevers family also owned Goat Castle in Dalkey, now Dalkey Heritage Centre, above which can be seen the Cheevers' flag, carrying the family crest of three goats. The goats tell us about the origin of the name Cheevers, which is derived from the French 'chevre', meaning goat. The Cheevers family were French-speaking Normans who had arrived in Ireland in the twelfth century.

The eighteenth century was a period of penal laws, when religious persecution against Catholics and Protestant dissenters continued. Records are scanty for this period, but Monkstown was within the Catholic parish of Loughlinstown with a population of 570 Catholics and 196 Protestants. A mass-house was reported in Cabinteely in 1731. In 1766, a religious census conducted by the vicar of Monkstown made reference to Fr John Byrne, parish priest, as '... a person of good character and well respected by both Catholics and Protestants', which suggests a degree of religious tolerance in the area.

THIS PAGE TOP *DUNLEARY OLD HARBOUR 1760–1836* BY MARGARET GOWAN
BOTTOM MAX CHIVERS (CHEEVER) OPPOSITE PAGE TAYLOR'S MAP, 1816

Reuniting the Cheevers Family

The Cheevers' family story has a contemporary twist. At the time of Walter Cheevers' expulsion from Monkstown, one of his sons went to America instead of accompanying his father to Connaught. This branch of the family lost contact with the Irish–English branch for many years. In 2001, representatives of the two branches met at Monkstown Castle, 348 years after the separation! This is the story, as told by Max Chivers, (the name has been spelt in a variety of ways), to a gathering at Monkstown Castle in April 2005:

When I visited Monkstown last in May 2001, it was to meet a descendant of Walter Cheevers, who was transplanted in 1653, when the building was vacated for General Edmund Ludlow. Legend has it that one of the Cromwellian soldiers levelled an insult at the statue or head of the Blessed Virgin and was immediately smitten with blindness. A younger son of Walter, called Thomas, set sail [for America] at the same time as his father set out for Connaught, and landed in Virginia. Although Thomas and another brother met in the US once, the 'Cadet branch of Monkstown' and the senior branch

had not met for 348 years. In fact, as far as we knew, all we had on Thomas was a full stop after his name, since all family papers were destroyed!

Monkstown Castle continued as a prominent residence for several more centuries. When it was put up for sale in 1788, it was described as the second-best residence in south Dublin, having a 91-foot high tower, a three-storey castle, a chapel, library and saloon, and it was surrounded by greenhouses. It even had an ice-house. Through marriage, it came into the possession of the De Vesci and Pakenham families, which have given their names to many of the streets in the area. During the nineteenth century, the castle fell into decline and is today reduced to two towers and a curtain wall.

The Nineteenth Century

The Monkstown we know today derives its character from its nineteenth-century development as a desirable residential suburb. It owes its popularity to two major developments: the construction of the harbour and railway to Dún Laoghaire. The effect of these two developments generated a building boom during which Monkstown was transformed from a sparsely populated country village to a prosperous area of terraces and squares, substantial private houses and impressive public buildings, creating the Victorian environment we see around us today.

History of the Harbour

There had been a harbour in the little fishing village Dunleary for many centuries, and the dún (castle), had been erected by Laoghaire, the King of Tara, above the estuary in the fifth century to secure the only inlet on the south side of Dublin Bay.

During the Middle Ages, Dalkey grew in importance and Coliemore Harbour became the harbour for Dublin. Because of a sandbar at the mouth of the Liffey, the port of Dublin was difficult to access for the increasingly large ships of the day, so goods and passengers were transported by road from Dalkey to Dublin. Dunleary had also become a port of some significance for traffic to and from England, but not of the same order as Dalkey. There is a record of the King's Deputy embarking from Dunleary in 1554 and General Ludlow of Monkstown Castle also used it. Other prominent travellers who passed through the port were John Wesley and Dean Swift, and, in 1776, Arthur Young the distinguished agriculturalist began his *Tour of Ireland* there.

The early harbour at Dunleary comprised the estuary and a harbour wall on the east side. By 1765, a proper pier had been constructed, but it was not a great success because of silting. The Coffee House stood on a high bank above the harbour and accomodated travellers.

A Tragic Double Shipwreck

Dalkey and Dunleary were effectively being used as harbours for Dublin, though some boats could proceed as far as Ringsend and disembark at the Pigeon House Hotel. However, if a ship got caught in a storm in Dublin Bay, there was no shelter and she was at the mercy of the elements.

This problem came to the fore in a dreadful double tragedy on 19 November 1807, when two troop ships, the *Prince of Wales* and the *Rochdale,* set out from the Pigeon House with soldiers who were going to fight Napoleon. Almost as soon as they left, a snowstorm with an easterly gale set in, making progress immensely difficult. The following morning they were still in the bay. The storm intensified and, in the end, the *Prince of Wales* was driven onto the rocks at Blackrock House which was then owned by Sir John Lees. The master, Captain Jones, launched the longboat, and ensured the safety of the ship's

crew, two soldiers and the steward's wife and child. The remaining 120 passengers were callously left to their fate and all were drowned.

The fate of the *Rochdale* was similar. She was driven along the coast burning blue lights and firing distress guns to attract attention. Local people had to dodge the flying bullets. Anchors were cast but the cables snapped. She finally struck rocks at Seapoint, beside the Martello Tower and all 265 on board were drowned. They were within 12 feet of land, but the storm was so fierce that they didn't know it.

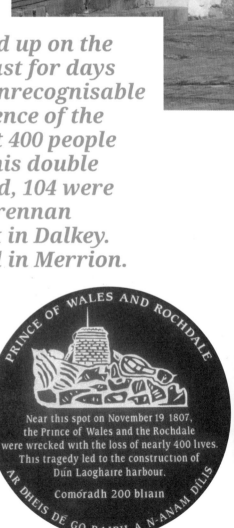

Bodies were washed up on the shore along the coast for days after. Many were unrecognisable because of the violence of the shipwrecks. Almost 400 people were drowned in this double tragedy. Of the dead, 104 were buried in Carrickbrennan Graveyard, and six in Dalkey. Others were buried in Merrion.

Captain Jones of the *Prince of Wales,* the mate and the steward were subsequently charged with murder, but the charges were dropped for lack of evidence.

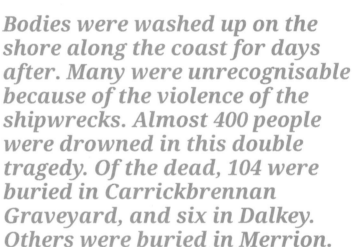

PRINCE OF WALES AND ROCHDALE

Near this spot on November 19 1807, the Prince of Wales and the Rochdale were wrecked with the loss of nearly 400 lives. This tragedy led to the construction of Dún Laoghaire harbour.

Comóradh 200 bliain

AR DHEIS DÉ GO RAIBH A N-ANAM DÍLIS

Public Outcry

The outcry that followed this double tragedy resulted in public pressure to construct an 'asylum' harbour at Dunleary, to enable ships going to Dublin to ride out a storm in safety, and to avoid the risks of the sandbar at low tide. A petition was drawn up at a meeting in Monkstown Parish Church in 1808. There was no urban or district council at the time and the parish vestry had considerable civic responsibilities. In 1811, a pamphlet was published by 'A Seaman' making a powerful case for the construction of a harbour at Dunleary, and rubbishing the rival port of Howth. In 1815, a further petition to parliament demanded the construction of a deep-water harbour south of Dunleary. The act authorising the construction was eventually passed in 1816 and work began the following year under the direction of Scottish engineer John Rennie. The East Pier was completed in 1821 and in that year King George IV embarked from the new harbour after a visit to Ireland. He gave the town a new name – Kingstown – to mark the event.

The West Pier was finally completed in 1859, and created the largest artificial harbour in the world. By that time, the sandbank that had so bedevilled shipping for centuries had been eliminated by the combined action of the South Wall and the Bull Wall, which created a funnel for the receding tide and scoured away the sandbank. This meant that large ships could enter Dublin Harbour without difficulty, rendering the new harbour at Kingstown redundant for its original purpose – providing shelter for ships caught in Dublin Bay during a storm.

OPPOSITE PAGE BOTTOM LEFT BLACKROCK HOUSE, HOME OF SIR JOHN LEES BOTTOM RIGHT COMMEMORATIVE PLAQUE FOR THE ROCHDALE AND PRINCE OF WALES SHIPPING DISASTERS THIS PAGE TOP MARTELLO TOWER, SEAPOINT BOTTOM ROCHDALE SHIPPING DISASTER SEAPOINT SHOWING THE MARTELLO TOWER

The First Commuter Railway in the World

A second major innovation of the period was to transform the landscape, both literally and metaphorically.

When the Dublin–Kingstown railway was first proposed, the intention was that it would be a freight service to bring goods that had been unloaded in Kingstown Harbour to Dublin. The railway was a relatively new technology, but it won out against the alternative argument to build a canal into Dublin. However, as we have seen, by the time the railway was built, there was no need for it to accomplish the original purpose. The railway was completed as far as the West Pier in 1834, and already the Dublin and Kingstown Railway Company had hit on a plan to

exploit a new market: they began to promote the railway as a commuter line, facilitating business people who wanted to work in the city but live by the sea. This was a new concept, and it was to prove profitable for the company. They also promoted sea-bathing and Blackrock baths were constructed beside the station. The company had completed a census of traffic on the Dublin road through Blackrock and observed the following over a period of seven months in 1831:

29,256 Private Carriages; 5,999 Hackney Coaches; 113,495 Private Jaunting Cars; 149,754 Public Cars; 20,070 Gigs; 40,485 Saddle Horses; 58,297 Carts.

It can be seen that there was a considerable amount of traffic on the road and the railway company believed that many of these travellers would choose to use the new service. By the same token, it can be imagined the devastation the trains caused to businesses associated with horse transport – not only the drivers and owners, but the farriers, the harness makers, the cart and carriage-makers. In time, the railway contributed to a change in architecture as well, as the practice of building stables also declined.

There were three classes of ticket on offer on the railway: first class was for the wealthy who wanted to travel in style and were prepared to pay for it; second class was for those who wanted to travel in comfort, but at a reduced cost; third class was for workers and the less well-off who wanted to come and go at the least expense possible. The railway was a boon for people working on the harbour, which was still under construction. Workers coming from Dublin paid half fare and this encouraged house building and ensured a steady stream of prospective customers for years to come. Special rates were also available for students, enabling families to settle while still having access to schools in the city. Excursion fares were available at weekends and on special occasions, such as the Kingstown Regatta, a visit by the naval fleet, boat races and firework displays.

Quakers had been associated with the development of railways in England and they were also involved in the new Irish enterprise. Local resident, Thomas Pim was a director of the Dublin and Kingstown Railway Company and James Pim Jr was company secretary and, later, treasurer.

As well as contributing to population growth, the railway changed the physical landscape. From Merrion, the railway leaves the land and crosses the bay on embankments. This is very evident at Booterstown where, today, a bird sanctuary occupies the area between the embankment and the original coast. Blackrock Park covers an area that was filled in, coincidentally covering the original Black Rock which gave the town its name. At Monkstown, it is still possible to visualise the embankment between the West Pier in Dún Laoghaire and Seapoint where the intervening space has been filled in, creating a more gradual descent to the sea and more pleasant vistas for house owners. The railway company did have great difficulty negotiating with some of the landowners who were very opposed to the new mode of transport, and Lord Cloncurry and the Rev. Sir Harcourt Lees of Maretimo and Blackrock House

respectively exacted a very large amount of money for their co-operation. The railway company also bought the Salthill Hotel because they required the land, and William Dargan, the engineer in charge, had his men cut back the cliffs at Salthill. Stations were built at Seapoint and at Salthill.

One of the effects of the railway was to cut off access to bathing facilities for local people and it was through the campaigning of Monkstown resident Charles Haliday that access was created by way of footbridges. There was also an elegant footbridge at the Salthill Hotel. Of course, Lord Cloncurry had ensured private access at Blackrock with his personal bridge and harbour constructed at the expense of the company. The railway company also saw some benefit and contributed to construction of bathing facilities and provided an all-in return ticket plus bathing during the summer months.

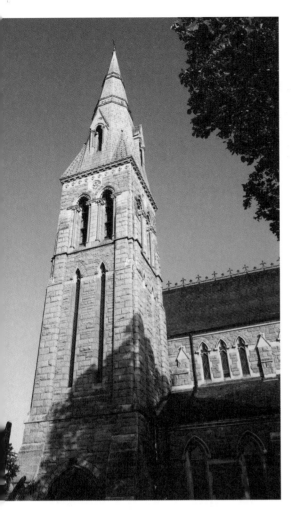

CLOCKWISE FROM TOP LEFT ST PATRICK'S ROMAN CATHOLIC CHURCH, MONKSTOWN; MONKSTOWN PARISH CHURCH; LECTERN, ST JOHN'S CHURCH MOUNTTOWN; PORCH OVER FRONT DOOR, THE MANSE, PRESBYTERIAN CHURCH YORK ROAD; FRIENDS MEETING HOUSE, PAKENHAM ROAD

The Church in the Community

As a resident community grew in Monkstown, institutions were established and public services were provided. The churches were at the heart of the community, particularly the Church of Ireland because of its legal position as the established church. Monkstown was an unusual parish in that it contained a high concentration of wealthy residents – merchants, industrialists and professionals, along with old colonial and services retirees. In the early nineteenth century, it was one of only a small number of Church of Ireland parishes with a growing congregation of well over 1,000. The foundation stone for the original church built in 1789 had been laid by the Lord-Lieutenant himself and the enlarged parish church of the nineteenth century was the largest Protestant parish church built in Ireland at that time.

The Church played a much broader role than just organising religious services. The parish vestry of Monkstown Parish Church was the small group of lay people who assisted in running the parish and, in the absence of local authorities, it had a large range of duties. In Monkstown, these duties ranged from road maintenance to the appointment of constables; from the supervision of public houses to the organisation of poor relief, and establishing and managing a school. One interesting duty was the erection and maintenance of stocks – the kind that you were locked into so that people could pelt you with rotten fruit! Sadly, they were required in Monkstown from time to time.

Ratepayers of all denominations in the parish could attend and vote at general vestry meetings where secular matters were discussed. The vestry also levied local taxes to pay for these services, which was not a popular part of their job. There was particular resistance among Roman Catholics, and non-conforming Protestants (Presbyterians, Quakers and Methodists) to taxes that went towards supporting the Church of Ireland. Collecting the tithe was particularly unpleasant, and there were 'Tithe Wars' throughout Ireland in the early 1830s. During that decade, legislation was introduced to relieve the vestry of responsibility for civil matters and the consequent obligation to raise taxes. This, and tithe reform in general, contributed greatly to the easing of tension. The Church of Ireland parish was no longer required to tax the whole population for its benefit and became solely a religious unit.

Separately and together, the churches played an important role in serving and forming their communities. They also demonstrated their Christian commitment in ways which were to benefit many others throughout Ireland and the world. This is a significant story of which Monkstown can be very proud.

A number of examples of faith in action, or practical Christian charity, in Monkstown stand out. It is remarkable that in a small parish, not one, but two, major missionary movements with a focus on health care, were founded that have

subsequently spread worldwide. These are the Leprosy Mission established by the Pim sisters Isabella, Charlotte and Jane, who lived on Alma Road and the Medical Missionaries of Mary established by Marie Helena Martin of Greenbank (which was demolished to make way for Carrickbrennan Lawn). Both of these organisations have contributed to the health and spiritual welfare of millions of people worldwide. Jonathan Pim who had also lived in Greenbank was joint-secretary of the Friends' Famine Relief Committee which did such good work throughout Ireland during the Great Famine. The local soup kitchen they established is marked by a plaque on the wall outside the Quaker Meeting House on Pakenham Road. In addition to the work of church organisations, there was the outstanding commitment to social justice by local residents Charles Haliday, who lived in Monkstown Park, and Dr William Plant of Monkstown Hospital.

There was also a commitment to missionary work in all the churches in Monkstown. Apart from those mentioned above, there were the Indian and Chinese missions of the Presbyterian Church and the Rev. Robert Warren Stewart's Church Missionary Society work in China. It is also interesting to see how the spirit of practical Christian charity and the commitment to missionary work evident in Monkstown during the nineteenth century has been continued into the twentieth century. Each year, many enjoy the performance of 'Messiah for All' at Christmas-time in Monkstown Parish Church. This is a lasting monument to the Rev. Billy Wynne who initiated the concert to raise funds for The Samaritans whose Dublin branch he established in 1970. Edel Quinn was to become the first envoy to Africa of the Catholic organisation the Legion of Mary and worked tirelessly in Kenya, Uganda, Nyasaland and Tanzania from 1936 until her death in 1944. She was following in a well-established tradition of Christian missionary work in Monkstown.

GOAL, now a major international humanitarian organisation that has saved countless lives in the developing world, was founded in 1977 by Monkstown resident John O'Shea, a former sports journalist. GOAL is in the tradition of the Leprosy Mission and the Medical Missionaries of Mary in its commitment to social justice.

CLINICS

SURGICAL	Tuesday	2.30 P.M.
GYNAECOLOGICAL	Monday	2.30 P.M.
EAR. NOSE & THROAT	Tuesday	10.30 A.M.
PSYCHIATRIC	Tuesday	9.00 A.M.
EXTERNAL DRESSINGS	Monday to Friday	9 TO 11 A.M.

Hospital and Orphanages

It was the 'Churchwardens of the Parish of Monkstown' who instigated the process that resulted in the establishment of Rathdown Fever Hospital in 1834, though a dispensary had been in existence on Monkstown Road since 1812. Their initial attempt had been rebuffed in 1831, but they persisted and their efforts undoubtedly mitigated the effects of the cholera epidemic that reached the area during the 1830s. The cost of running the hospital in the 1840s was £150 per annum and their resources were stretched and there were frequently two or three patients in a single bed! During the Great Famine, the 'sick poor ... were humanely and skilfully treated'. The original hospital had sixteen beds and, by 1848, this had increased to thirty-two. It was extended again in 1880 and its capacity was increased once again.

OPPOSITE PAGE TOP LEFT ART EXHIBITION VILLAGE DAY, 1989 TOP RIGHT EDEL QUINN WHO DIED IN NAIROBI IN 1944 MIDDLE SIDE GATE ST PATRICK'S CHURCH BOTTOM PRESBYTERIAN CHURCH, YORK ROAD THIS PAGE MONKSTOWN HOSPITAL, PAKENHAM ROAD

Monkstown Hospital, as it had become, was blessed in the distinction and longevity of its medical officers: Dr William Plant (1835–1875), Dr Joseph Beatty (1878–1919), and two generations of de Courcy-Wheeler, Robert (1919–1956) and his son Desmond (1956–1987). It continued to serve the community until it was closed in 1987 in an early bout of rationalisation.

completely inadequate. Mortality was high among the poor and there were many orphans in the area. There was little legislative protection for children – the Chimney Sweepers'

The conditions of the poor during the nineteenth century were very harsh and for the orphaned poor, they were appalling.

Work on the harbour and the railway had attracted many labourers, but work had ceased on these major projects by mid-century. There was no industry and while there was a considerable amount of house and church building, sanitary conditions were poor and basic amenities, such as water and lighting, were

Act forbidding the use of children to clean chimneys was only passed in 1875 and the Society for Protection of Children wasn't established until 1884.

The Society of the Daughters of the Heart of Mary founded an orphanage in Tivoli Road in 1860. The order of nuns had been founded in France at the time of the Revolution and their desire was to live in the community with no distinguishing habit, devoting their lives to prayer and good works. The founder of the Irish orphanage was Mary Anne O'Farrell from Kildare.

The intention had been to dedicate the orphanage to St Vincent and St Elizabeth and a large statue of St Vincent de Paul was ordered from France. But when the shipment arrived it was found to contain a statue of St Joseph! Thus did St Joseph become patron of the orphanage. The orphanage included a school, which was recognised as a national school in 1927 and was opened to all local Catholic children shortly afterwards.

In 1960, the orphanage was looking after seventy-three children. It remained in existence until 1983, and has since been demolished. The associated retreat house was bought by the Eastern Health Board of the time. The school, however, does continue in existence, as St Joseph's, and a community of nuns remains in residence.

The Cottage Home for Little Children was established on Tivoli Road in 1879 by Miss Rosa Barrett. Miss Barrett was English and had accompanied her brother to Ireland in 1874. She took an interest in the conditions of the poor and formed the view that many women could go to work in domestic service and improve their circumstances if they had a way of also minding their children. She initially established a day nursery, one of the first crèches to be established in these islands. She also provided residential care for some children, creating the first children's home in the United Kingdom of Britain and Ireland to cater for children younger than six years of age. Given the demand, it was found necessary to build a new home, which was opened in 1887, on a new site on Tivoli Road, at the north end of Royal Terrace. Miss Barrett continued in charge until 1920 when she retired, though she did remain as president until her death in 1936.

OPPOSITE PAGE TOP THE COTTAGE HOME FOR LITTLE CHILDREN, TIVOLI ROAD. BOTTOM BIRDS' NEST ORPHANAGE, YORK ROAD. THIS PAGE TOP CLASSROOM MPC WITH HEADMASTER MR ROUNTREE BOTTOM WILLIAM PLANT, FIRST DOCTOR AND SURGEON, MONKSTOWN HOSPITAL

The Smylys of Dublin were a devout and philanthropic family. Mrs Ellen Smyly (née Franks) had founded a day school for poor children in Townsend Street in 1852. Over a period of years, she established a number of orphanages for boys and girls, including the Birds' Nest on York Road in 1862. The Birds' Nest was established 'for the education and support of Roman Catholic children, whose parents and guardians had consigned them to its care'. This was viewed in some Catholic quarters as proselytism. Associated with the Bird's Nest were Mrs Whately, the wife of the Most Rev. Dr Richard Whately, Archbishop of Dublin, and their daughter Mrs Wale, who are commemorated in an inscription on the outside of the building. Originally, the Smyly Homes were supported entirely by charitable donations, and the Smyly family was intimately involved with them for more than a century. In the 1970s, they began to receive state funding. There are still two Smyly homes in Monkstown – Glensilva and Racefield House – which provide residential care services for boys and girls aged twelve to eighteen. Ellen Smyly was a personal friend of Dr Barnardo.

Some Monkstown Schools

Monkstown Parish School

In an education census conducted in 1824, thirty-two schools were identified in the 'barony and parish of Monkstown' attended by almost 1,000 pupils. These included Monkstown School, beside the parish church, which had been established as early as 1791 and remained in operation until 1986. The school was established to provide an education for 'the Children of every Denomination' and was funded by public subscription and an annual charity sermon. It was also supported by the Association for Discountenancing Vice, which Catholics objected to.

parish and the children of wealthy families would have had private tutors in their homes.

The Hall School

The Hall School is remembered fondly by former students. It was established as a Ladies' College in 1872, in numbers 2 and 3 Belgrave Square (today Comhaltas Ceoltóirí Éireann uses the buildings) by a Miss Towell and her sister, Mrs Daly.

In 1898, Joseph Vaughan bought the school for his two daughters, Henrietta and Colletta, and it became the Vaughan Hall School. The school grew and additional

Monkstown School was well funded and well equipped, and teachers were paid a decent salary by the standards of the time. With the introduction of a non-denominational national school system in 1831, funding was provided by government to approved schools.

Many of the schools identified in the census were small private 'pay schools' run in private houses. There were many private schools in the

premises were acquired in number 33 Belgrave Square. St Grellan's, at 61 Monkstown Road, was acquired and its spacious grounds were used

Christian Brothers' College

The Christian Brothers established a school on Eblana Avenue in Dún Laoghaire in 1856. In 1928, they bought Fairyland, which had been built as his family's own home by John Semple Senior. In 1985, when the order closed the provincialate in St Helen's at Booterstown, it was moved to Fairyland which was renamed St Helen's.

for sports. In 1929, Lily Colletta Vaughan became headmistress and she contributed greatly to the further success of the school. She established the Past Pupils' Union of 'Old Hallites' and improved the accommodation and sporting facilities at St Grellan's.

In 1954, the Hall School came under the Department of Education and the mews to the rear of the buildings in Belgrave Square were developed as science laboratories. In 1965, a further house, Hollybrook House in Queen's Park, was purchased

for use as a junior boarding school. Senior girls lived in Belgrave Square and 'middle boarders' lived in the annexe to St Grellan's. Miss Vaughan retired in 1972, after forty-two years as principal. The Hall School merged with Park House School in 1973 and was renamed the Park Hall School. During the following year, the school had two principals, Miss Catt and Miss Mew! The Park Hall School then merged with Hillcourt School to become Rathdown School.

The Christian Brothers opened a secondary school at 6 Tivoli Terrace in 1949, but the space was inadequate and the Brothers negotiated with the Longford and de Vesci estates and with Dún Laoghaire Corporation to buy Monkstown Park, the former home of Charles Haliday, the humanitarian. The Corporation was involved because there had been plans to establish a public park in the area. Monkstown Park had been used as a boarding school 'for the sons of gentlemen' in the early years of the twentieth century and continued to prepare students for British public schools until its closure in 1945. When the Christian Brothers acquired the school, they renovated the building extensively. Successive renovations over the intervening period have completely transformed the original building.

THIS PAGE TOP CHRISTIAN BROTHERS' SCHOOLBOYS PROCESSING DOWN CARRICKBRENNAN ROAD BOTTOM CARDBOARD CLOCK, MONKSTOWN PARISH SCHOOL OPPOSITE PAGE TOP DRAIN, THE HILL BOTTOM PIPE & BRICKWORK, KNOX HALL

Urban Development

The rapid growth in the population of the area around Monkstown was not matched by the provision of public utilities. There was increasing demand for services and facilities to provide residents with a good quality of daily life. Monkstown was not a township in its own right, but as Dún Laoghaire (Kingstown) and Blackrock developed, services were gradually improved.

Water and Sewage

The water supply and sewage systems were completely inadequate and contributed to the repeated outbreaks of cholera during the nineteenth century. Charles Haliday, that great champion of the poor in the area, was loud in his criticism of the public authorities and landlords for the unsanitary conditions that prevailed in poorer areas. Many private houses would have their own well, and it was the coachman's job to pump water to the storage tanks.

For generations, the people of Monkstown and the surrounding area depended on fresh water from Juggy's Well, which was located just next to Monkstown Hospital on Pakenham Road at the junction with The Hill. The original name may have been Jacob's Well and it was reputed to have been a holy well containing

a sacred trout! Water carriers made a living transporting water around and even the ships of the Royal Navy relied on it.

However, during a prolonged drought in 1868, Juggy's Well dried up, causing great distress. It wasn't the only public well in the area but it was the most important. The authorities were finally moved to act and a number of schemes were looked at to solve the water problem. Eventually, it was decided to link in with the new Dublin city scheme that would draw water from the Vartry river at Roundwood. This scheme was overseen by Sir John Grey, chairman of the Dublin Corporation Water Works Committee, who, in a spirit of public service, bought up the surrounding land at Roundwood to prevent speculators getting their hands on it and then sold it to Dublin

Corporation at cost. He was knighted in 1863, and his statue stands in O'Connell Street at the junction with Abbey Street. By linking in with the Dublin Corporation scheme, a reliable water supply became available and at a much lower cost than an independent scheme. The connection to Monkstown was made in 1869.

It was 1880 before an adequate sewage system was installed, pumping untreated sewage well out into the bay. Further improvements were made in 1894, when John R. Wigham, the distinguished lighthouse engineer, was chairman of Blackrock Urban District Council. Because of these improvements, the foreshore became safe for bathing and sailing. Today, it would be unacceptable to discharge raw sewage into the bay, no matter how far out, but it was only relatively recently that the pumping station at Salthill was installed to pump sewage to the treatment plant in Ringsend.

Electricity

Several local private and commercial institutions installed their own electricity generators in and around the turn of the twentieth century: the Royal Marine Hotel was one of the first in 1897; the Salthill Hotel soon followed as did Monkstown Hospital in the 1920s. The West Pier Generating Station was established by the Urban District Council using four diesel generators, and supplied Monkstown. In 1925, a local generating station was constructed on the West Pier, but it only lasted four years, before being taken over by the ESB at the request of the Urban District Council. Local generators were being phased out and were being integrated into a national grid.

It is interesting that to take account of people's ability to pay, a service was provided in some poorer areas whereby a proprietor paid one shilling (about 6 cent) per week for a limited supply of 100 watts, enough to run a single light and a radio! It was unmetered, but the supply was cut off when the limit was reached.

THIS PAGE LEFT LAMP POST, TRAFALGAR LANE RIGHT LAMP MONKSTOWN PARISH OPPOSITE PAGE LEFT DOMESTIC GAS FITTING, TRAFALGAR TERRACE RIGHT GAS LAMP STANDARD, MONTPELIER MANOR

Gas

A number of gas companies were established in Dublin in the 1820s to generate gas from coal. In the late 1820s, the Hibernian Gas Light Company secured the contract for the public lighting of Dublin, the Dublin–Kingstown railway and, it appears, Kingstown and Monkstown. Some of the old lamp standards can still be seen, for example, above the post box on Temple Hill, at the end of Longford Terrace and outside private houses on Montpelier Parade.

The first gas works in Monkstown was established beside the Coal Quay by the Kingstown Gas Company in 1864. At the time, it was quite common for large towns all over Ireland to have their own gas companies providing public lighting. Over time, following the Alliance and Dublin Gas Consumers Act of 1866, these many gas companies were amalgamated and the small local companies disappeared, eventually being replaced by the Commercial Gas Company of Ireland.

The Introduction of Trams

When the railway was established in 1834, it competed with the private, horse-drawn traffic along its route. There was still plenty of business for the hackney drivers however, as the train had a fixed route. Horse-drawn trams became available in Monkstown in 1883 when the Blackrock and Kingstown Tramway Company was set up. The trams ran down Monkstown Road, passed along the Crescent and Cumberland Street to Kingstown. It was now possible to travel from Dublin to Dalkey by horse-drawn tram, in three hours and with three changes of car. The railway company had nothing to worry about, as it could travel the same distance in thirty-five minutes!

In 1893, the Imperial Tramways Company, an English concern, bought the Blackrock and Kingstown Tramway and electrified the line. On the 16 May 1896, the line from Ballsbridge to Dalkey was ceremoniously opened.

The new electric tram caused some disturbance to churchgoers in Monkstown and the select vestry wrote to the manager of the Electric Tramway Company a few weeks later complaining about the 'ringing of bells during services when passing church'! The fare from Kingstown to Dublin was 3 old pence (about 1.5 cent). It was to prove very successful, and continued to pass through Monkstown village until the 9 July 1949.

THIS PAGE TOP OPEN-ROOFED TRAM PASSES MONKSTOWN PARISH CHURCH MIDDLE TRAM STANDARD STILL UTILISED TODAY BOTTOM DUBLIN ELECTRIC TRAMWAYS OPPOSITE PAGE ROYAL VISIT OF KING GEORGE V AND QUEEN MARY, MONKSTOWN 1911

Royal Visits

From the beginning, Kingstown, and by extension Monkstown, was associated with royal visits. Indeed the route from Kingstown through Monkstown to Dublin was sometimes referred to as 'the royal route' by Dubliners. The town of Dunleary was renamed Kingstown in honour of the visit by George IV in 1821, whose departure was commemorated in an obelisk on the seafront. In fact, his embarkation was somewhat undignified as the king was, in the words of one commentator, 'speechlessly drunk, and suffering from a distressing looseness'. Subsequent royal visits were much more respectable.

In 1849, just a year after the uprising by the Young Ireland movement and while the country was still reeling in the aftermath of the Great Famine, Queen Victoria visited Ireland accompanied by Prince Albert and four of her children. The purpose of her visit was to give a boost to Ireland's economic development.

On 2 August, she went to Cork where she gave the name Queenstown to Cobh. The royal yacht then visited Kingstown on 5 August where the Queen disembarked for Dublin. The Queen received a very enthusiastic welcome as she progressed through Kingstown and Monkstown on her way to the city and to the Vice-Regal Lodge in the Phoenix Park, now Áras an Uachtaráin. She attended a variety of gala events and banquets and impressed a great many with her youthful vitality and happy demeanour. At the most important reception of her visit in Dublin Castle, she wore 'a superb pink Irish poplin dress decorated with gold shamrocks', which received many compliments.

As well as visiting many places of note in Dublin, she visited Mount Anville, the home of William Dargan the leading promoter of the Dublin–Kingstown railway. He declined her offer of a knighthood.

Queen Victoria also visited Ireland in 1853, when she opened the Great Exhibition held on Leinster Lawn, the brainchild of the same William Dargan, and again in 1861 and finally in 1900, when she received a rapturous reception in Monkstown. Some locals sought to make money from the event, with windows being 'hired ... for smart figures'.

King Edward VII visited twice, in 1903 and in 1907 accompanied by Queen Alexandra. On the first occasion, his visit was intended to counterbalance the nationalist celebration of the centenary of Robert Emmett's rebellion in 1803. The royal procession through Dublin was reported to have attracted a smaller crowd than the Emmet commemoration. There was no official welcome from Dublin Corporation.

In 1907, after an address of welcome had been delivered by Kingstown Urban District Council in the Pavilion, the party proceeded to Dublin via the Crescent and

Monkstown Road to visit the Irish International Exhibition in the RDS. They then carried on to the Vice-Regal Lodge in the Phoenix Park to attend a reception. The royal party returned to Kingstown and stayed on the royal yacht overnight, before attending the races at Leopardstown the following day. The king was most unhappy on his visit to Dublin Castle to find that the crown jewels had been stolen. They have never been found. The royal couple set off for Cardiff on 12 July.

On 7 July 1911, King George V and Queen Mary visited. On their arrival a 21-gun salute was fired from Killiney Hill, which was also specially illuminated for the occasion. The weather was described as 'tropical'. The grounds of the Pavilion were decorated with Japanese lanterns hanging in garlands and hundreds of lights burned brightly in lamps set out on the parterre. In the harbour, the yachts of the Royal Navy were also decked out in bunting. The royal party was greeted on Victoria Wharf by the Lord-Lieutenant. Following an address of welcome, the party proceeded in open carriages towards Monkstown via Cumberland Street and the Crescent. The boundary of Blackrock Township extended as far as Monkstown Parish Church, and it was there that the royal visitors were presented with a second address of welcome, this time by the Blackrock Reception Committee. Several large grandstands had been erected alongside the church and opposite the Knox Hall to accommodate hundreds of dignitaries and onlookers. A floral arch spanned the road bearing the slogan 'Céad Míle Fáilte' and the road was bedecked with bunting and flowers.

Interestingly, in their address, Blackrock Town Council detailed the improvements they had made in providing accommodation for working-class people, including the new drainage scheme for the town, the new public park and the new Technical School providing for 300 students. This was an indication of the increased civic consciousness of the time. The royal party then proceeded on to Dublin Castle for a gala reception. Their visit lasted for three days and included a visit to the Phoenix Park races and to St Patrick's College in Maynooth where they were received by Cardinal Logue. The party returned to England via Kingstown on 13 July. It would be a long time before Ireland would have another royal visit.

The Early Twentieth Century

The Decade of Revolution

We are accustomed to the nationalist narrative of the decade of revolution 1913–1922, but a study of Monkstown gives us an opportunity to see another side of the picture. In Monkstown, there was a large Protestant community who had a strong attachment to the crown and to the union with Britain. For them, the Home Rule debate that was conducted during 1913 and 1914 was a source of great anxiety. They were opposed to Home Rule and their attachment to the crown is evident in the warmth of the welcome they gave to royal visitors in the early part of the twentieth century and in the letter of condolence dispatched by the select vestry on the death of King Edward VII in 1910. However, the social composition of the community had changed, and as early as 1900, there had been a nationalist majority in Blackrock Urban District Council.

The Home Rule Bill was passed in 1914, the crowning historical achievement of the Irish Parliamentary Party in Westminster, but its implementation was postponed for a minimum of twelve months on the outbreak of the First World War. During 1914, there was a threat of civil war in Ireland with arms being imported illegally by the unionist Ulster Volunteer Force in April 1914 and by the nationalist Irish Volunteer Force in July 1914.

WAR MEMORIAL WINDOW MONKSTOWN
PARISH CHURCH 1920

When Britain declared war in August 1914, a general call for volunteers was made. The Protestants of Monkstown volunteered in large numbers, principally out of loyalty to the crown and the union. Many Catholic nationalists also volunteered with their own motives – some were idealistic, others were looking for adventure and others again wanted to escape the poverty in which they lived.

The 1913 Lockout had compounded the poverty of many and induced some to join up. The poverty of Dublin and the circumstances of the poor during and after the 1913 Lockout are described in James Plunkett's *Strumpet City*. John Redmond, leader of the Irish Parliamentary Party, urged the Irish Volunteers to join, and he himself lost a brother in the war. In 1915, it was estimated that out of a population of 17,000 in Kingstown, 1,100 men were serving in the British army. There were also 400 from Blackrock.

The recruitment campaign targeted existing groups of friends who had associated in civilian and sporting life. When Lt Col. Geoffrey Downing, commanding officer of the Royal Dublin Fusiliers and former captain of Monkstown Rugby Club, appealed to rugby players, he got an enthusiastic response, and 'D' Company included a large group from Monkstown and Kingstown. There was also a recruiting station in George's Street. In some local communities – Brookfield Buildings in Blackrock and the village of Kilternan for instance – large

numbers of young men volunteered. In Monkstown's Church of Ireland parish, 155 men and women volunteered, of whom twenty-eight never returned. Among the dead were six sets of brothers, including the two sons of the rector of Monkstown, Canon John Clarence Dowse, and two clergymen. Several died in the appalling slaughter of Gallipoli. Five members of the Presbyterian congregation on York Road were also killed. A memorial to the twenty-eight parishioners who died was unveiled to their memory in Monkstown Parish Church in 1920. A further memorial in St John's Church, Mounttown, was dedicated to the fifteen young men from that parish who died. It comprised a double stained-glass window and a brass plaque listing their names. These memorials were removed to Monkstown Parish Church when St John's closed in 1985.

There are no records of how many Catholics from the parish joined but, proportionately from the rest of the country, as many Catholics as Protestants enlisted. It is estimated that more than 200,000 Irishmen joined the armed forces at this time. Two brothers of Marie Helene Martin from Greenbank enlisted one of whom died, and Marie Helene herself volunteered as a nurse, serving in Malta and in France. There is no memorial to the Catholics from the parish who fought and died in the war. This is mainly because the 1916 Rising and its aftermath left many nationalists afraid to draw attention to their participation on behalf of the British in the war, and so families didn't seek to

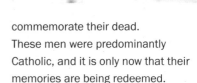

commemorate their dead. These men were predominantly Catholic, and it is only now that their memories are being redeemed.

Monkstown Hospital was used as a military hospital during the war, and several large houses, including Monkstown House and Dunedin (on Monkstown Avenue, now demolished), were used as convalescent homes for soldiers. Elizabeth Wright Jones, matron of Monkstown Hospital (1906–1920) was awarded the Royal Red Cross for her services during the First World War and was the only Irish nurse from what would later become the Free State to receive it. The Jolley family donated a field at the top of Monkstown Avenue to the British authorities as a recreation space for injured servicemen, which became known as the Soldiers' and Sailors' Field. It is now a sports ground.

TOP RMS LEINSTER MAILBOAT AT KINGSTOWN, TORPEDOED 1918 BOTTOM CONVALESCENT FROM THE FIRST WORLD WAR AT CORRIG CASTLE

On 10 October 1918, a dreadful tragedy struck when the Royal Mail service ship the RMS Leinster was torpedoed by a German submarine just outside Dublin Bay with the loss of at least 501 lives. Although the ship carried mail (some of those killed were civilian postal workers, sorting letters in the hold), there was also a large number of military personnel and nurses on board. The majority of those lost came from Kingstown and Holyhead, to where the ship had been sailing.

During the Easter Rising, Kingstown was the landing point for British troops sent to quell the fighting. The soldiers advanced through Monkstown – along the route taken a few years earlier by royal visitors – towards the city and, for two weeks Monkstown, like other suburbs was cut off. In Monkstown Parish Church, the time of the Sunday evening service was changed from 7 p.m. to 6 p.m. during May on account

of the rebellion! The subsequent War of Independence did not have much impact on Monkstown. The 1920 Government of Ireland Act established the Irish Free State as a dominion within the Commonwealth. The attitude of many is summarised by the approach of Lady Dockrell, a former chairperson of Blackrock Town Commissioners.

'Although a confirmed unionist, the late Lady Dockrell has accepted the new conditions created by the Truce [Treaty] in 1921 and warmly co-operated with the new government.'

The Civil War that erupted in 1922 caused the emergence of very bitter divisions throughout Ireland. Several Protestant families in Monkstown felt it necessary to leave for their own safety, among them was Dr Robert Lynn Heard whose four sons had fought in the war.

It is only in recent past that nationalist Ireland has been able to acknowledge the sacrifices made by all the men and women who volunteered for service during the war years. In the words of President Mary McAleese, speaking at the opening of the Island of Ireland Peace Park on 11 November 1998:

'In this generation, we redeem their memory, acknowledging their service and the pain of those who loved them.'

The Second World War

For the citizens of Monkstown, the Second World War was not as traumatic an experience as the First World War. By the time the war started in 1939, Ireland was an independent, neutral state. Members of the Monkstown community did enlist, and some were killed during conflict, but not in the same numbers as in the First World War and without the same extreme conflict of loyalties.

There is one anecdote from the Second World War that is worth repeating. The fact that the headquarters of the German Legation was in Gortleitragh in Monkstown meant that there was a certain amount of security activity in the area throughout the war. A German spy, Hermann Goertz, landed in Ireland with the purpose of liaising with the IRA.

However, he had great difficulty making contact with the German ambassador, Dr Edward Hempel, until the ambassador hit on the idea of having a party to which he could invite a large number of people, among whom Goertz wouldn't be noticed. In the course of the evening, the ambassador repeatedly absented himself to meet privately with his special guest. Goertz was captured in 1941 and spent the remainder of the war in Arbour Hill and the Athlone Barracks. At the end of the war, he lived locally for a while and applied for political asylum in Ireland. This was denied and when he was on the point of being extradited, he committed suicide by swallowing a phial of prussic acid.

Gortleitragh was where De Valera called to express his condolences on the occasion of Hitler's death.

THIS PAGE TOP SUBWAY FROM GARDEN OF GORTLEITRAGH TO WILLOW BANK, THE SLOPES BOTTOM GRAVE OF GOERTZ AT THE GERMAN CEMETERY GLENCREE OPPOSTIE PAGE TOP GORTLEITRAGH HEADQUARTERS OF THE GERMAN LEGATION DURING THE SECOND WORLD WAR BOTTOM PLAQUES COMMEMORATING THE ROBINSON BROTHERS, MONKSTOWN PARISH CHURCH

In
EVER LOVING MEMORY
OF
DOUGLAS ST QUENTIN ROBINSON
PILOT OFFICER, ROYAL AIR FORCE
MISSING 6TH AUGUST 1938, WHILST FLYING ON DUTY.
AGED 21 YEARS.

"UNDERNEATH ARE THE EVERLASTING ARMS."

IN
EVER LOVING MEMORY
OF
KENNETH BASIL ROBINSON
FLYING OFFICER, ROYAL AIR FORCE
KILLED IN ACTION 7TH JUNE 1944
AGED 22 YEARS.

"O VALIANT HEARTS, WHO TO YOUR GLORY CAME."

Modern Monkstown

In the second half of the twentieth century, Monkstown experienced a second building boom, large enough to compare with the early Victorian period. New developments in Monkstown Valley, Castle Park, Richmond Park and Monkstown Farm greatly increased the population and filled up much of the available green space. Some heritage buildings were demolished to make way for multistorey apartment blocks in Queen's Park and The Slopes as well as small developments being inserted in the extensive grounds of other early buildings. Carrickbrennan Lawn was built on the site of the Sacred Heart School, which had occupied two historic buildings, Yapton and Greenbank. Salthill Apartments were constructed on the site of the old Salthill Hotel.

This has been achieved, fortunately, without losing the Victorian atmosphere of area or encroaching on the early architecture, with the terraces and squares and pleasant avenues. This is due in no small measure to the vigilance and efforts of resident associations and of An Taisce who fought a dogged battle on occasion. Richmond Park is a particular example: permission had been granted for its demolition in 1987, but after a sustained campaign the house was saved.

The 2000 Planning Act protects architectural heritage in law and thankfully, older houses are not being destroyed mindlessly as often happened in the past.

The County Council has also played its part with the appointment of two Conservation Officers and a Heritage Officer, an example to other counties. The combination of residential and commercial activity in village communities is an objective of the county development plan, and it works in Monkstown.

Nonetheless, not all developments are desirable and some mistakes have been made. Some developments are out of character. Mistakes have sometimes been made out of carelessness when interesting artifacts are cast aside or ignored: the horse trough at the junction of Mounttown and Knapton Road has vanished, and Victorian steps and gate piers at the entrance to the lateral park on Seapoint Avenue have been discarded. Juggy's Well has been filled in and adjacent stepping stones over the stream have been covered over. There is a general carelessness about details that add interest – gate piers, old street-lamp brackets and, importantly, old street signs. There is a variety of these signs dating from Victorian times and they are interesting artefacts in their own right, as well as having practical utility.

Homeowners can be equally culpable through carelessness and a lack of awareness. It is unquestionably difficult to maintain the character of an older dwelling and meet modern standards of insulation and sustainability. The County Council might consider an educational programme in the conservation of old buildings and their associated artefacts, such as iron railings, stucco, repairs to woodwork, sash windows and insulation. Sustainability in an old building would be an interesting series to add to the council's imaginative heritage programme.

Monkstown occupies a unique place with a definite character and architectural style, zealously guarded and viewed with deep affection by its residents. The old village centre at the Ring retains its village charm with its churches and community-scale retail sector. New businesses in recent years have complemented the existing atmosphere, making Monkstown a convivial and friendly place to live and relax.

Traffic management is a challenge and this can be expected to increase with development of housing on the old Dún Laoghaire golf course. It is worth remembering that the introduction of the railway and of trams also caused a measure of controversy in their time. There will always be a tension between preserving local amenities and allowing new developments and constant vigilance is called for to ensure that the community voice is heard.

Community matters. Monkstown is primarily a vibrant community of people, a village with a diverse and fascinating past, and a delightfully built environment. Modern Monkstown is also old Monkstown. We must look after it.

THIS PAGE TOP RICHMOND PARK HOUSE, c. 1987 MIDDLE STUCCO CEILING WORK, LONGFORD TERRACE BOTTOM SALTHILL APARMENTS ON THE SITE OF THE SALTHILL HOTEL

AT THE TIME OF THE FAMINE IN 1848
FOOD PREPARED IN A KITCHEN
BEHIND THIS WALL
WAS DISTRIBUTED TO THE NEEDY
THROUGH A WINDOW HERE.

CHAPTER 2

The Buildings of Monkstown

In the Middle Ages, Monkstown Castle was the centre of social and political life of the area stretching from Dalkey to Booterstown. The Monkstown we know today, however, was largely created in the nineteenth century, when it grew as a residential area between the developing urban and commercial centres of Blackrock and Dún Laoghaire (which was known as Kingstown at the time). It became an area of substantial houses occupied by landowners, successful business people and wealthy professionals. The architectural style is predominantly Victorian, along with a small number of earlier buildings. Peter Pearson describes the residential development of Monkstown as taking the form of 'middle-sized houses, most of which were detached, and generally built in the safe classical style, being stucco-fronted [a type of outdoor plaster], and often employing Georgian motifs such as the pillared door case and fanlight'.

There was considerable technological development during the nineteenth century and this was reflected in buildings. Mass-production and mass-transit made ornamental parts affordable – lots of brackets, spindles, scrolls and other machine-made building parts were used. It was a confident time with the expansion of empire and a succession of military and naval victories, which also found expression in architecture.

The population of Monkstown grew rapidly during the middle of the nineteenth century: in 1831, the aggregate population of Monkstown civil parish was 11,200; in 1861, it was over 30,000. This surge gave rise to huge demand for housing for all classes, which resulted in a great variation in housing conditions. *Saunders' Newsletter* commented thus:

'A notable fact with respect to all the recently built houses in the whole district [Dún Laoghaire area] is the rapidity with which they let. Many of them are let before they are roofed.'

The building boom lasted until the 1870s before it began to fall off. In the 1880s, the population stopped growing, rents fell and the population profile became increasingly older. Before the building of the railway, the coastline of Monkstown was rugged with low cliffs skirting the bay, as can be seen in Rocque's map of 1756. The estuary at old Dunleary was the only such inlet on the south coast of the bay and was the reason for the original location of the Dún of King Laoghaire, as well as the early harbour. The railway was constructed on an embankment and the subsequent infill created a much more graduated descent to the sea, creating a pleasant residential landscape with sea views.

The road network has also changed. In the early years of the nineteenth century, Seapoint Avenue was constructed to provide access to the Martello Tower, but the coast road from Clifton Terrace to Seafield Avenue along present-day Seapoint Avenue was not constructed until 1936. Monkstown Road was the principal thoroughfare with avenues descending to the sea.

TURRET, ST ANNE'S, THE HILL

Squares and Terraces

Monkstown's terraces and squares contribute greatly to its characteristic atmosphere, for residents and for those passing through, by train or by road.

Montpelier Parade was constructed about 1800 and is named after the French city of the same name. The houses built here had an uninterrupted sea view until Belgrave Square, Eaton Square and Alma Road were built in the latter half of the century. The houses were not commissioned, but built on a speculative basis and sold by the builder after construction.

The houses are three storeys over a basement and are relatively unadorned, though they are elegantly proportioned and still retain many period features. Quite a few of the street-lamp brackets remain on the house railings and there is a small 'green' with several original granite bollards separating the houses from the road.

There were originally several other buildings which carried the Montpelier name: Montpelier House (later Shandon) and Montpelier Manor. The distinguished broadcaster Charles Mitchel lived in the mews building of Montpelier Manor. Painter and historian Peter Pearson also lived on Montpelier Parade during the 1980s.

Longford Terrace is one of the most dramatic terraces along this coastline. It was constructed in two sections: the first section of fourteen houses, farthest from Dún Laoghaire, was constructed by 1842, and the second terrace with its distinctive retaining wall was built over the next decade. The developer was Thomas Bradley and the architect was George Papworth, with the terrace being named after the ground landlord, Lord Longford.

The houses are very substantial, three storeys over a basement with delightfully proportioned interiors. They are fronted by attractive cast-iron railings. Coach-houses, which would soon disappear as a feature of house design with the advent of the railway, were built to the rear of the houses, facing Monkstown Crescent. Today, these coach-houses contain various retail outlets.

The original lease stipulated that the land in front of the Longford Terrace houses should not be built upon, and it is now a public park and car park for commuters. With Brighton Terrace and Clifton Terrace, Longford Terrace presents a most impressive set of seafront buildings.

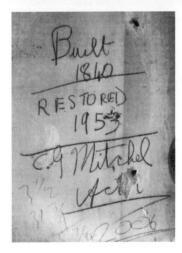

OPPOSITE PAGE TOP LONGFORD TERRACE, 1980S **BOTTOM LEFT** FRONT DOOR WITH FANLIGHT, MONTPELIER PLACE **BOTTOM RIGHT** MONTPELIER PARADE **THIS PAGE TOP** MONTPELIER PARADE, 1980s **BOTTOM** CHARLES MITCHEL LIVED IN THE MEWS OF MONTPELIER MANOR

Longford Place is an altogether more modest terrace. It is brick built, two storeys above a basement and facing away from the sea. The doors have fanlights and a window surround in stucco.

Trafalgar Terrace was completed in 1855, the golden jubilee year of the battle after which it's named. It was built by Daniel Crowe and probably to the design of John Skipton Mulvany on land leased from the Rev. Sir Harcourt Lees of Blackrock House, the son of John Lees, the notorious secretary of the Irish Post Office. Mulvany was the architect for the Dublin and Kingstown Railway Company.

Pearson describes the terrace as being 'designed with clean, simple lines and ornamented by simple features such as window recesses and slightly projecting porches which are decorated with brackets and victory wreaths'.

The original leases prescribed that tenants were not permitted to convert their premises into 'a Nunnery, Roman Catholic or Dissenting Chapel, Public Hospital, Infirmary, Mill, Iron Foundry, Distillery, Brewery, Shop or Tavern or to the place of trade of slaughter man, boiler, melter of tallow, tallow chandler, butcher, baker, victualler, blacksmith, farrier or nightman scavenger'. This was probably because the reverend landlord held very strong opinions on anything that diverged from orthodox Protestant teaching.

Brighton Vale was built during the 1840s on a narrow strip of land between the railroad and the sea. It forms an attractive terrace of villas and, though each has its own detail, overall the terrace retains a distinctive harmony in the use of decorative stucco and cast-iron railings. Number 5 is thought to have been the home of J.S. Mulvany, who is also believed to have been responsible for this design of the terrace.

THIS PAGE TOP CEILING ROSE AND LIGHT, TRAFALGAR TERRACE **BOTTOM** CONSERVATORY, BRIGHTON VALE **OPPOSITE PAGE MAIN IMAGE** COAL CELLAR, TRAFALGAR TERRACE **INSET** LONGFORD PLACE, FORMERLY WEBSTERS BUILDINGS

Belgrave Square was constructed over several decades, beginning in the 1840s when eight large terraced houses were built on the south side by John Semple Junior. Semple was also the architect of Monkstown Parish Church (Church of Ireland). Two of the houses were joined together to form the Hall School before it moved to St Grellan's on Monkstown Road (they now house Comhaltas Ceoltóirí Éireann). It had been Semple's intention to complete the square, but he was declared bankrupt in 1849 and that effectively finished his career. In the 1850s, houses were built on the west side and a long terrace of seventeen houses was constructed on the north side. The square was completed in the 1860s and was a very fashionable residential area in Victorian times, as indeed it is today! The coach-houses of Belgrave Square south backed onto Monkstown Road and have since been renovated as residences.

Eaton Square was laid out in the 1860s when four houses were built. The rest were built later by Thomas Dockrell of the well-known builders' supply firm. He also built a house for his own family which he named Camolin, after his home village in County Wexford. Camolin was demolished to make way for Scoil Lorcáin, Ireland's first gaelscoil. The Dockrells were prominent in public affairs and Lady Margaret Dockrell was chairman of Blackrock Urban District Council for a time. She was the first woman to be elected to Dublin County Council along with Hannah Sheehy Skeffington and was a leading figure in the movement to secure the parliamentary franchise for women.

Queen's Park is a delightful cul-de-sac off Monkstown Road, which originally comprised eight detached houses surrounding a particularly fine villa called Inismaan. The houses were developed in the late 1860s by Alfred Gresham Jones who, himself, lived at Inismaan. Riversdale House is an exceptional late Victorian mansion in Queen's Park, which was built by the Duff Egans, the Dublin wine and tea merchants, and is now owned by the Opus Dei religious order.

The Hill off Pakenham Road, is laid out in the form of a crescent on what used be a brickfield. Tudor Hall and Tudor House were built here in the early 1840s in a Tudor idiom, with elaborate granite porches and mullioned windows with small panes of glass. The most striking house on The Hill is St Anne's built by the architect William Caldbeck as his own residence. He incorporated many decorative features into its design, including a turret with an octagonal pointed roof and elaborately patterned slating.

CLOCKWISE FROM TOP LEFT HALL SCHOOL, BELGRAVE SQUARE SOUTH; NORAH LOVE, LOCAL RESIDENT, ON THE STEPS OF HER HOME, BELGRAVE HOUSE; WALNUT TREE EATON SQUARE; RIVERSDALE HOUSE, QUEEN'S PARK; CLENCHED FIST GATE HINGE, ST ANNE'S THE HILL

De Vesci Terrace was completed in 1846 as a 'superior terrace' with the arms of the Vesey family, displayed over the central pediment. Named after the ground landlord (the Vesey family held the title Viscount de Vesci), it was laid out with pleasure gardens, which incorporated tennis courts for the residents. The houses here display large, elegant bay windows and porticos supported by fluted Doric columns, and would originally have had a view over Dublin Bay. The terrace presents as a single integrated architectural unit. Finished in stucco, the original building leases stipulated that each house be painted 'Portland stone colour and none other' every two years, under a penalty of £5.

Grosvenor Terrace is one of the smaller terraces of Monkstown with two-storey houses over a basement. It takes its name from Grosvenor House, which stood where the apartment block of the same name stands today. The doors have an attractive semi-circular stucco detail picked out in white which contrasts with the brick walls. At basement level, the walls are built of polygonal blocks of granite, while the first and second storeys are made of brick. The unity of the terrace is greatly enhanced by the artfully crafted granite capstones on the garden walls and piers, with cast-iron panels in the walls.

Cambridge Terrace on York Road was built about 1865 and was one of the first terraces built of machine-made brick, which was beginning to supplant stone in house construction. These houses have an attractive wooden canopy over the door and have dormer windows.

OPPOSITE PAGE INTERIOR, THE HILL **THIS PAGE TOP RIGHT** GROSVENOR TERRACE **BOTTOM RIGHT** CHIMNEY POTS AND DORMER WINDOWS, CAMBRIDGE TERRACE **TOP LEFT** NUMBER 1 DE VESCI TERRACE **BOTTOM LEFT** POLYGONAL GRANITE FACING ON BASE OF HOUSES, GROSVENOR TERRACE

Tobernea Terrace was also built in the 1850s on the site of Seapoint College. The houses have three storeys with a large bow, affording wonderful sea views at all levels. An interesting double dormer window provides a quirky detail above the two central houses.

Tobernea gets its name from tobar ní (the washing well) – the actual well was in the small adjacent park.

Ardenza Terrace, which was built in the 1850s on the site of Seapoint House, has imposing entrance gate piers. The houses are three storeys over a basement and have an uninterrupted view of the sea over a shared green area.

Alma Road was laid out in 1855 on the grounds of Temple Hill. The name may come from the involvement of the solicitor and developer Thomas Alma, or from a commemoration of the British victory of the battle of that name in the Crimean War (1854).

OPPOSITE PAGE, CLOCKWISE FROM TOP LEFT NUMBER 1 TOBERNEA TERRACE, OVERLOOKING THE SEA; GOTHIC STYLE WINDOW, TOBERNEA TERRACE; ENTRANCE TO ARDENZA TERRACE **THIS PAGE CLOCKWISE FROM TOP LEFT** BALNOOTRA, ALMA ROAD, DESIGNED BY ARCHITECTS DEANE AND WOODWARD; LIGHT STANDARD, ALMA ROAD; ORIGINAL HOUSE NAME, ALMA ROAD; DECORATIVE ENTRANCE PORCH, ALMA ROAD

The Villas of Monkstown

From the early 1830s, a very distinctive villa-style house was being constructed in the coastal area stretching from Kingstown northward through Monkstown to the village of Sandymount.

These little symmetrical houses, detached, semi-detached and terraced, have classical features and are built in a style almost unknown in Britain.

Some of these houses are single storey, but in the characteristic double-storey house a flight of about eight steps, with handsome railings leads to a distinguished front door often with columns and a fanlight.

A long window is set on each side of the door and a hipped roof directly over it sometimes with a parapet.

Below the door is a string course, and beneath it, the two shorter windows of a semi-basement continue the lines of the windows above.

THIS PAGE, CLOCKWISE FROM TOP VILLA STYLE HOUSE, THE CRESCENT; ORIGINAL DOOR LATCH, THE CRESCENT FROM 1835; DETAIL OF DECORATIVE IRONWORK **OPPOSITE PAGE, CLOCKWISE FROM TOP RIGHT** RICHMOND HILL WITH WISTERIA, SEAPOINT AVENUE; LETTERS FOR ALBANY

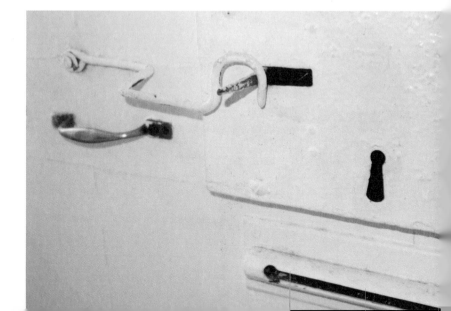

Monkstown Crescent is possibly the earliest example of this style. Built in 1836, some are one-storey; others have a basement. The doors have fanlights and sidelights. The villas of the Crescent face the former stables of Longford Terrace, which are now used for a wide range of retail services.

Richmond Hill, comprising eight houses, was laid out in 1836 and several of the houses are in a similar villa style to Monkstown Crescent – single-storey villas with reception rooms at the entrance level, over a basement accommodating the kitchen and additional bedrooms. They are delightfully proportioned inside and out.

When they were constructed, several of these houses were occupied by Quaker families. Other examples of the villa house-style can be found on the avenues of Monkstown: Oriel Lodge on Seafield Avenue, The Albany on Albany Avenue, Laurel Lodge on Brighton Avenue. These avenues were built in the first half of the nineteenth century and contain some of the finest houses in the area. The street names are redolent of gracious living in the elegant English seaside towns of the period. Along Seapoint Avenue, further examples include Annesley and Santa Maria. The latter was a subject of controversy in 1981 when the owner obtained planning permission to demolish the villa and replace it with apartments. The planning permission was rejected on appeal to An Bord Pleanála.

Auburn Villas on Carrickbrennan Road also date from this period.

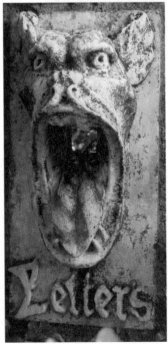

Seapoint Avenue was not completed until the 1930s when the section between Albany Avenue and Seafield Avenue was constructed. The earlier footpath along the cliff top was named Adzar Passage after a house of that name that had stood there formerly.

Detached Private Dwellings

A number of early houses were built along what was called Dunleary Ridge, a crescent of high ground stretching from the top of Monkstown Avenue, where it meets Stradbrook, along the line of the present Monkstown Avenue, past the Castle and St John's Church in Mounttown and along Tivoli Road. In the early days, this would have provided a fine view of Dublin Bay. Monkstown Avenue was laid out in the late eighteenth century, and the names of early buildings, which have since disappeared, are retained in street names: Dunedin and Ashton are examples.

Rockford Manor on Stradbrook Road is a fine granite house built by Sir William Betham and later radically renovated in the Tudor style by William Bruce. It was, until recently, the home of the Presentation Sisters who established the girls' school of that name there. The motto carved on the wall reads 'Nisi Dominus Frustra' ('It is in vain without the Lord').

Windsor stands at the top of Monkstown Avenue. Originally constructed in the late eighteenth century, it has been much altered since. It originally faced the mountains but was rebuilt to face the sea and Monkstown Castle during the Victorian era. In the early nineteenth century, it was owned by William Lane who gave his name to Lanesville. The stockbroker Thomas

Pim also lived there for a time. Today, Windsor houses a children's crèche. Opposite Windsor an ex-soldier turned dairy man, who had survived the 1882 Battle of Tel-el-Kebir in Egypt, established a dairy of that name. It was later managed by the Sutton family and was taken over by Premier Dairies. The name is still retained in the nearby T.E.K. football club.

Monkstown House was built in 1859 and is distinguished by its fine proportions and tall Italianate tower of Dalkey granite. Built for the merchant prince, William Harvey Pim, no expense was spared in its construction. It boasts a fine portico and a remarkable entrance hall and staircase. It was used as a military hospital during the First World War and is now a community centre.

Monkstown Castle is the name of a private house that causes some confusion with the actual castle close by. It was built in the early 1800s probably for Jonathan Pim, who lived there and who offered the grounds for the establishment of Dublin Zoo in 1829. At the time, the surrounding lands were known as Monkstown Castlefarm and extended to Mounttown. The grounds included the ornamental pond and island on the stream at the back of the medieval castle.

De Vesci Lodge, opposite the entrance to Monkstown Castle, at the top of Carrickbrennan Road, was the Dublin residence of the Viscount de Vesci of Abbeyleix, a local landlord.

Next to it stood a house belonging to Lord Ranelagh, which was demolished by the historian and humanitarian Charles Haliday to make way for Monkstown Park, which he built to accommodate his growing library, including an immense collection of documents related to Irish history. This building is now incorporated into Christian Brothers' College.

OPPOSITE PAGE, TOP MOUNTTOWN HOUSE, DEMOLISHED IN 1966 TO MAKE WAY FOR FITZGERALD PARK BOTTOM ROCKFORD MANOR, HOME OF SIR WILLIAM AND MOLYNEUX BETHAM THIS PAGE, CLOCKWISE FROM TOP RIGHT ELEGANT CAST-IRON STAIRCASE RAIL, MONKSTOWN HOUSE; SOMERSET LATER BLACKROCK RFC, DEMOLISHED 1988; TEK DAIRY ADVERTISMENT ON A FORD PREFECT; LAUREL BANK, OFF LANESVILLE

Glandore in present-day Glandore Park was built about 1850 by William Vesey, brother of Viscount de Vesci (the viscount was also the Second Baron Knapton), and was designed by Deane and Woodward in the Venetian Gothic style. Today, it is very much hemmed in by modern housing. William Vesey was also largely responsible for the building of St John's Church, Mounttown, and gave his name to Vesey Place situated off York Road. Willow Bank, facing Vesey Place was constructed in 1865, a terrace of substantial semi-detached houses.

Fairyland was built about 1804 by the architect John Semple Senior as his family home. When built, it had an uninterrupted view of the sea. Given that it was Semple's own house, it is remarkably simple in design, with little external elaboration.

Local historian Étain Murphy, has drawn attention to the similarity between the corbelled fan vaulting of the entrance hall and that of the ceiling in the parish church. Though on a much smaller scale, the hallway suggests in embryonic form what was to emerge so spectacularly in Monkstown Parish Church, designed by the younger Semple at a later date.

Fairyland was bought by the Christian Brothers in 1928 and renamed St Helen's in 1985 when they moved from a building of the same name in Stillorgan.

Along Monkstown Road, several early houses, some of them early nineteenth century, have survived the depredations of modern development.

These include Dalguise, Easton, Beauparc, Drayton, Purbeck, Marino, Clifton and the Priory. Hills Borough, now Berrington, is reputedly the oldest house in Monkstown. It has been suggested that John Semple Sr was the architect for a number of these buildings.

Gamble's Lodge on Mounttown is named after 'the widow Gamble', a rather shadowy figure who may or may not have existed, but who reputedly revealed the whereabouts of a priest on the run to the authorities during penal times. It is also suggested that she was a witch! The building may have been a dairy associated with the de Vesci estate.

Mounttown House was demolished in 1966 to make way for Fitzgerald Park. It had been the home of Jonathan 'Jonty' Hanaghan the distinguished psychoanalyst. He presided over 'The Group' which met regularly to explore the relationship between Freudian psychoanalysis and Christianity.

Richmond Park built about 1874 was generously left to the Cheshire Homes in 1980 by Mrs Mary Briscoe. It was subsequently at the centre of a planning controversy in 1987 and was saved by an An Taisce campaign.

Several gate lodges have also survived and there are also some remarkable gate piers, Heathfield with its stags' heads being a fine example. Elm Lodge has interesting ironwork on its parapet. It was the residence of the Reverend Nangle, during a brief period as curate in Monkstown. He founded o the Achill Mission in 1834. Dr Plant, successively the medical officer to Monkstown Dispensary, and a doctor and surgeon in Monkstown Hospital, named his house Plantation. Today, it is called Gortmore. The small building with unusual chimneys at the entrance is the original Monkstown Dispensary over which Dr Plant presided until the hospital was opened. Melbeach (originally Mill Beach), off Albany Avenue, was for many years the home of the Findlater family. There were Findlater shops in Blackrock, Kingstown and Dalkey and the family played an important role in community life as Kingstown Town Commissioners.

CLOCKWISE FROM TOP LEFT VENETIAN GOTHIC STYLE, GLANDORE HOUSE; BLUE DOOR, MONKSTOWN ROAD; STAG'S HEAD AT HEATHFIELD, MONKSTOWN ROAD; GAMBLE'S LODGE; FAIRYLAND, NOW ST HELEN'S; VINCENT QUILTER AT DALGUISE

The Churches of Monkstown

Between 1830 and 1870, there was a tremendous flurry of church building in the Kingstown area: twelve churches (six Church of Ireland, five Roman Catholic and one Presbyterian), the Friends' Meeting House and a Wesleyan Chapel were built during this period. Added to this, the capacity of Monkstown Parish Church was almost quadrupled to 1,200 in 1831, and was further enlarged in 1862. This suggests that Monkstown had a very devoted community of Christians! It was also a very busy time for builders.

It is worth observing that the architects and masons of the time believed not only that a church should be a place of worship, but should also in itself be an offering to God. Consequently, these buildings display craftsmanship of a very high order.

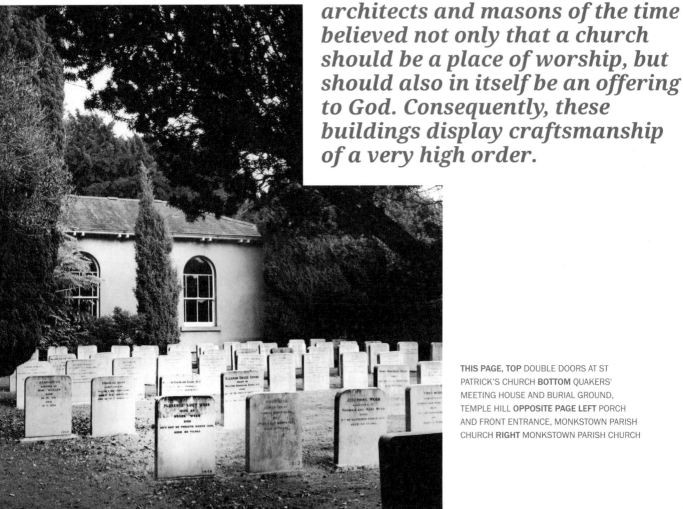

THIS PAGE, **TOP** DOUBLE DOORS AT ST PATRICK'S CHURCH **BOTTOM** QUAKERS' MEETING HOUSE AND BURIAL GROUND, TEMPLE HILL **OPPOSITE PAGE LEFT** PORCH AND FRONT ENTRANCE, MONKSTOWN PARISH CHURCH **RIGHT** MONKSTOWN PARISH CHURCH

Monkstown Parish Church

Unquestionably the most recognisable and distinctive building in Monkstown is Monkstown Parish Church on the Ring, which has been an object both of controversy and of great affection since its construction. *The Dublin Penny Journal* of 1834 declared that 'there is not a spot in the church where the eye could rest without pain', Sir John Betjeman in contrast described it as one of his 'first favourites for its originality of detail and proportion'. It is a wonderfully idiosyncratic mix of architectural styles.

When the earlier church in Carrickbrennan Graveyard could no longer accommodate the area's growing population, a new site was chosen for a parish church. This first building was completed in 1789. It was a simple rectangular church with a square tower and was described at the time as 'the fairest country church in Ireland'. It stood in open ground surrounded by fields that swept down to the sea. It accommodated a congregation of 340 but, by 1818, it was described as 'always much crowded', and given that construction of the new harbour in neighbouring Dunleary had only just begun, it could only become more crowded. Monkstown church was 'the only church from Ringsend to Bray ... an extent including eleven populous villages and a very thickly inhabited countryside'.

As the population continued to grow, the church was extended at the instigation of Archbishop William Magee to the design of the architect Joseph Semple Junior. Two large transepts, galleries and a large east end were added. He ornamented the façade with the 'chessmen' which make the building so remarkable. He also added a lantern to the earlier square tower.

All this was accomplished amid much controversy and changes of plan. Archbishop Magee asserted that he had complete authority to direct the architect and builder as he wished and he frequently by-passed the local Building Committee, causing much confusion and resentment.

The renovated church was opened for Divine Service on Christmas Day, 1831 with a capacity for 1,200. A further modification was introduced in 1862 with the addition of a chancel on the east side to meet new liturgical requirements.

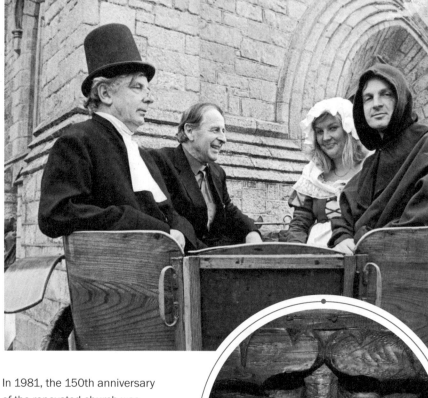

The architect for this was John McCurdy who accomplished the task so sensitively, and in keeping with the earlier Semple design, that it is difficult to distinguish the new from the old. The interior of the church is also worthy of comment: its spectacular ceiling, corbelled fan vaulting and scalloped plasterwork echo the Moorish air of the exterior. The imaginative plaster colouring also adds a wonderful warmth to the atmosphere.

In 1981, the 150th anniversary of the renovated church was celebrated by broadcasting a service on national radio. The bicentenary of Monkstown Parish Church was celebrated in 1989, culminating in a very successful 'Village Day'. Roads were closed and all the Christian churches joined in the celebrations. Prominent on the day in a horse-drawn carriage were Rev. Kevin Dalton in his stovepipe hat and Fr. Vincent Quilter.

The Knox Hall was built in 1904 through the generosity of Alice Chaloner Knox of Silverton in Monkstown, to commemorate her husband Captain Edward and their nephew Eustace. It was to be the parochial hall for Monkstown parish. The architect was Mr Richard Chaytor Millar, with offices in Great Brunswick Street, and Christopher Jolley was the builder. The building is constructed in neo-Tudor style. The large window facing Monkstown Road displays the arms of the Knox family and the motto 'Moveo et Proficio' ('I move and I prosper'). In the 1970s the Rev. Billy Wynne, rector, used the small meeting room in the hall as the *Friendly Room*, a drop-in centre for anyone who needed company and a cup of coffee.

Monkstown Parish School was built in 1791 shortly after the completion of the new church and remained in use until 1986. It was a originally a parish school for all denominations with accommodation for the teacher upstairs and classrooms downstairs. It displays a classic Georgian façade, simple and dignified. A notice reads: 'Monkstown Primary School 1791'.

OPPOSITE PAGE, CLOCKWISE TOP LEFT KEYHOLE TO SAFE 18TH CENTURY; VESTRY INKSTAND, MONKSTOWN PARISH CHURCH; L TO R THE REV KEVIN DALTON, FR VINCENT QUILTER, DIANE SWIFT AND JOHN EDMONSTON, VILLAGE DAY, 1989; GREEN MAN CARVING, COMMUNION TABLE, MONKSTOWN PARISH CHURCH; BRICKWORK AND GRANITE CEILING IN THE VAULTS, MONKSTOWN PARISH CHURCH THIS PAGE, CLOCKWISE TOP RIGHT SIDE VIEW KNOX HALL; MONKSTOWN PARISH SCHOOL; HANDLE FOR LOWERING LIGHTS, KNOX HALL

St Patrick's Church

When the Catholic parish of Kingstown was constituted in 1829, it included Monkstown, which only became a parish in its own right in 1902. St Patrick's was built along much more traditional lines than the Church of Ireland Monkstown Parish Church. It was described at the time of its dedication in 1866 as 'an architectural gem' in the French style with Gothic features of the fourteenth century. The spire was added later and completed in 1881. The architects were Edward Pugin and George Ashlin.

Augustus Pugin was, more than anyone else, responsible for the adoption of the Gothic Revival style as the national style of Victorian Britain, and he transformed architecture in Britain and Ireland. The most celebrated of his buildings is the Palace of Westminster, which incorporates the British Houses of Parliament and Big Ben. Ashlin managed the Irish office and Irish commissions at a very busy period of church building in the Irish Catholic Church. Among other local churches, the firm also designed St Joseph's in Glasthule and the Sacred Heart Church in Donnybrook. Michael Meade, of Westland Row was the builder. He had also built the Town Hall in Kingstown.

As with Monkstown Parish Church, plans were changed several times during construction and there was trouble with the building workers. The Incorporated Bricklayers of Kingstown objected to workers from Dublin being engaged on the building on the basis that the church was being built with local funds. Richard O'Carroll, chairman, and John Hickie, secretary, signed the formal protest letter. The matter was eventually resolved and building proceeded.

Cardinal Cullen laid the foundation stone in 1861 and dedicated the church in 1866. Tickets of admission to the dedication were sold to raise funds, ranging in price from £1.5.0 to 2 shillings and sixpence. Tickets were available from Miss Beamish's in Upper George's Street in Kingstown. Haydn's 'Imperial Mass No. 3' was performed and 'all the celebrated amateurs of Dublin and Kingstown have kindly promised their assistance to the distinguished professional performers Mr Croft [musical director for the occasion] has engaged'.

THIS PAGE, TOP LEFT DECORATIVE RAILINGS AND PIER, ST PATRICK'S CHURCH TOP RIGHT REV. ROBERT CANON EATON BOTTOM ST PATRICK, ST PATRICK'S CHURCH OPPOSITE PAGE CORPUS CHRISTI PROCESSION, 1950s

The walls of St Patrick's are of local rusticated granite faced with Bath stone. There is a fine rose window of Caen stone on the north side and, above the entrance, there are sculpted panels depicting scenes from the life of St Patrick. There is extensive use of decorative stone in the interior: shafts of red Cork marble support the chancel arch, columns of Mitchelstown brown porphyry divide the nave from the aisles, and black Ennis limestone and white Italian marble are also used. Michael O'Connor was responsible for the stained-glass windows.

St John's Church, Mounttown

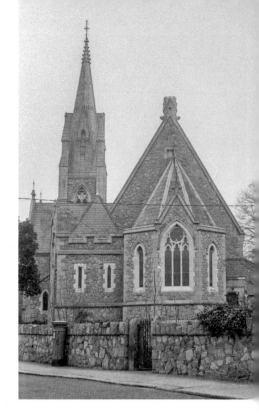

St John's Church was built at the instigation of the Hon. William Vesey, who had recently taken up residence in his magnificent new house, Glandore. Building a new Church of Ireland church so close to Monkstown Parish Church was problematic, but the necessary permissions were granted and the church opened for divine worship on 23 May 1860. Welland and Gillespie were the architects and their original building was rectangular in shape, the transepts and chancel were added later, giving the church a cruciform shape. An interesting feature of the construction is the use of polygonal stone in the lower part of the side walls. This is sometimes referred to as 'hock and ham' stonework. The church was closed in 1983 and sold in 1985 to the Society of St Pius X, a Catholic organisation that resumed its use for divine worship. When the church was sold, many of its artefacts, including the altar, stained-glass windows (among them a war memorial window) and its wall-mounted memorials were removed to Monkstown Parish Church.

The Friends Meeting House

There was a significant number of Quaker families living in Monkstown in the nineteenth century. Prominent among them was the Pim family, several of whom had substantial houses locally. Other early Monkstown Quakers included Alexander, Barrington, Bewley and Chandlee. Monkstown Quakers were merchants and industrialists. By the late 1820s, there were enough in the community to hold local meetings in Seapoint House, where Ardenza Terrace now stands. Quakers were to the fore in the development of the railways in Ireland. Thomas Pim was the first chairman of the Dublin and Kingstown Railway Company, and James Pim was secretary and later treasurer. Construction of the Monkstown Meeting House began in 1832 to the design of George Papworth. It was extended for the first time as early as 1837. Further changes were made in 1968 and in 1998 the caretaker's lodge was replaced. The Meeting House is a modest, unpretentious structure completely lacking in ornamentation, reflecting Quaker belief. The fine ceiling and structural roof timbers are of Oregon pine. These replaced the earlier roof destroyed in a fire in 1880. On the perimeter wall, there is a plaque to mark the location of a soup kitchen held there during the Great Famine. The building is wonderfully illuminated with natural sunlight through its very large windows. The Quaker graveyard is nearby on Temple Hill.

THIS PAGE, TOP ST JOHN'S CHURCH, MOUNTTOWN BOTTOM RIGHT OREGAN WOOD CEILING, FRIENDS' MEETING HOUSE BOTTOM LEFT FRIENDS' MEETING HOUSE, PAKENHAM ROAD OPPOSITE PAGE TOP PRESBYTERIAN CHURCH, YORK ROAD BOTTOM OLD CHURCH, CARRICKBRENNAN GRAVEYARD

Presbyterian Church

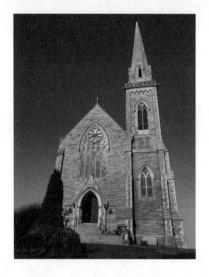

The Presbyterian Church on York Road was built in 1863 to replace an earlier building opposite the current site known as the 'Scots Church'. The earlier building was much more modest and had been constructed originally to cater for the substantial number of Scottish workers who came to work on the new harbour. When the new church was built, the older building housed the Kingstown School for a period until 1968 when Kingstown School amalgamated with Avoca School Blackrock, to eventually form Newpark Comprehensive School. It is now used as a training centre.

The church has a dramatically different architectural style to the earlier church with its gothic windows and elegant spire, and is very similar to Rathgar Presbyterian Church. Both were designed by Andrew Heiton and built by Gilbert Cockburn. Alex Findlater who resided nearby was a generous benefactor. In 1834, he had opened an Irish and Scotch Whiskey Store and High Class Grocery on Lower George's Street, where Penneys stands today. The same Alex Findlater built the church on Parnell Square popularly known as Findlater's Church.

A delightful feature of the interior is the beautiful inscribed mosaic tablet which was placed over the vestry door in 1929 in memory of the Rev. F. Stuart Gardiner. The church hall is in the spacious church basement. During the First World War, a large number of Scottish fishermen arrived in Kingstown with their trawlers to undertake mine-sweeping duty. They received great hospitality from the congregation in York Road and the church hall was used as a recreation and reading room.

The name of the church was changed in 1972, from Kingstown Presbyterian Church to Presbyterian Church, Dún Laoghaire. The presbytery is also an interesting building with an attractive canopy over the door.

The Church Ruin in Carrickbrennan Graveyard

Local legend has it that there has been a church on the site of the present ruin in Carrickbrennan Graveyard since the year 798 when the monks of Inish Patrick fled the Vikings, bringing with them the relics of their founder St Mochanna. There is no documentary or archaeological basis for this claim. Any original wooden building would have been replaced with a stone structure in the tenth or eleventh century. During the Reformation, the church was stripped of any elaborate decoration to conform to the Protestant liturgy and by the time Edward Corker rented the castle from Walter Cheevers in 1667, the church was reported to be 'in a ruinous state'. Corker restored the church and signed it with his initials and the date: 'EC 1668'. In 1723, the church was still in good repair, and was well maintained for most of the eighteenth century, according to the vestry records. In 1787, however, it was declared that Carrickbrennan church was no longer adequate for the congregation and 'out of repair'. The decision was taken 'to build a large and handsome Church in a more convenient location'. When the new church was built, the old church was allowed to fall into ruin. The building did have a brief return to life during the nineteenth century, when it was partially restored to serve as a shelter for night-watchmen, guarding the graveyard against body-snatchers, a lucrative trade at the time.

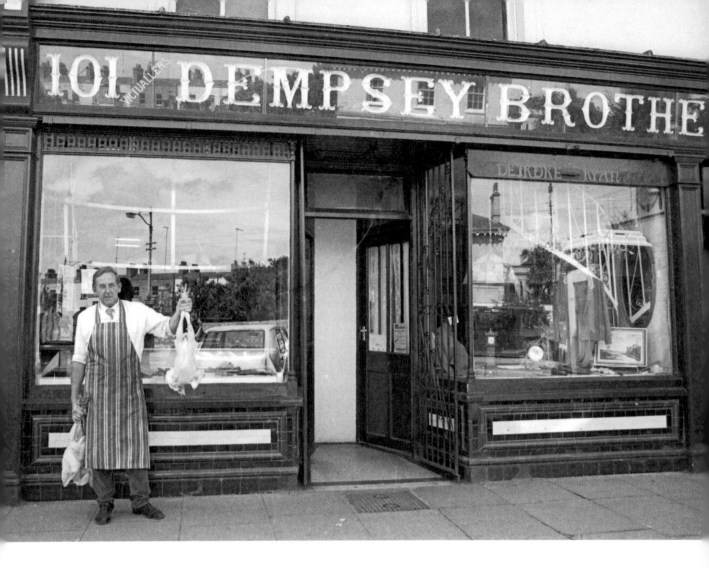

The Victorian Village

Unlike its neighbours, Blackrock and Dún Laoghaire, there are no large office blocks or shopping centres in Monkstown, which has retained the atmosphere and scale of a residential village. The shops are small with easy pedestrian access. Many of them have an inclusive community feel, where shoppers enjoy a conversation with neighbours while transacting their business. There are very fond memories of earlier shop proprietors among older Monkstown residents, and many anecdotes. John Lindsay Cobbler, Lee's Knitwear, Tyndall's (later Wraps) and The White Shop have all gone but live on in memory.

There are two distinct clusters of shops and businesses in Monkstown: one centred on the Ring and extending up Carrickbrennan Road; the other along Monkstown Crescent. The former constitutes the heart of the old village dominated by the spires of the adjacent churches and the shop architecture reflects the nineteenth-century village atmosphere.

There are several well-preserved shopfronts with interesting architectural detail. The original hand-carved Dempsey Brothers sign in gold lettering of number 101 is an example. Dempsey Brothers

had bought the business from the Field Brothers, who were well known victuallers, in 1916. William Field was a nationalist MP and was also very prominent in local politics. He receives honourable mention in James Joyce's *Ulysses* for his role as chairman of the Irish Cattletraders and Stockowners Association. Number 105, Cosgrove's Pharmacy, previously Lane McCormack, has retained the interior of the old shop.

The name Goggins is associated with the nineteenth-century family who excelled in bog-oak sculpture. Cornelius Goggin moved from his native Killarney to set up business in Nassau Street, Dublin, in 1851. He was very successful, secured a royal warrant and amassed a sizeable fortune. He built a substantial house in Booterstown and purchased several properties in Monkstown. His son, also Cornelius, set up a wine

An interesting feature of several shops is the unusual mosaic on the doorstep: 'Salve' ('in good health') at the entrance to number 103, lets us know that this was the location of the original Lane McCormack pharmacy – still a suitable greeting in a flower shop, with a wonderfully preserved shopfront.

Another such mosaic is 'Halliday & Co' at the entrance to number 91. Halliday & Co. was a general grocery and is now a laundry.

and spirit business in one of the Monkstown properties inherited from his father. Ellen Mary Goggin, the youngest daughter of Cornelius

Goggin carried on the bog oak carving business in Nassau Street with considerable success. She lived for many years at Hollyville

OPPOSITE PAGE, **TOP** PAT DEMPSEY OUTSIDE HIS SHOP, *c.*1988 **BOTTOM** WRAPS FORMERLY TYNDALLS NOW GREENES **THIS PAGE TOP** 'SALVE' - ('IN GOOD HEALTH'), ENTRANCE TO GREENE'S FLOWER SHOP **BOTTOM** THE ORIGINAL LANE MCCORMACK CHEMIST

House, 3 Carrickbrennan Road. The original Goggin's was a grocery and public house with three counters, including one for the bacon slicing! At Christmas-time, grapes were a great treat, arriving in barrels and packed in crumbled cork to prevent the grapes being crushed!

The bottom of Carrickbrennan Road is part of this little cluster with more small village shops. Older residents remember that the present post office was once Eltons Dairy and Roberts' grocery shop. Dairy produce, milk, butter and so on were delivered from their farm on Pottery Road.

CLOCKWISE, FROM TOP LEFT THE FIRST BLOOMSDAY AT GOGGIN & CO., 16 JUNE 1954; INTERIOR, MISS JENNINGS CHEMIST SHOP; G BYRNE'S, 1950, NOW HEWETT'S SHOP; JOHN LINDSAY'S COBBLERS SHOP; AUSTIN AND AGNES ROBERT'S ELTON'S DAIRY NOW POST OFFICE; MICHAEL (JOHNNY) LAWLOR, ONE HORSE POWER; MEANYS ICONIC YELLOW SHOP, SEAPOINT AVENUE

There was another local dairy run by the three Lawlor brothers from their farm in Alma Place behind St Patrick's Church. There is a family legend that a Lawlor ancestor swam across Dublin Bay to Howth in 1761, the year of George III's coronation!

The presence of not one, but two letterboxes suggests that residents have been busy correspondents. In the late nineteenth century, there were as many as five collections a day, six days a week, with one collection on Sundays. It was possible to send a letter, receive a reply, and respond, all in the one day!

Carrick Hoover Centre has a fine traditional shop front with the entrance set back and security gates attached. There is also interesting brickwork detail at first-floor level. The entrance doors have the original brass handles. Locals remember it as earlier housing both a haberdashery and post office, run by Mrs Scully and Miss Boyd respectively. It was by all accounts a delightfully old fashioned place, with stamps and postal orders being sold alongside pink knickers and long johns. Hewett's convivial newsagency was formerly Byrne's

and replaces an earlier building on the site. There were market gardens on the east side of Carrickbrennan Road in living memory.

The second retail cluster is on Monkstown Crescent, where a large number of businesses have opened in what had originally been the stable buildings of Longford Terrace. Many of these businesses are high-quality specialist outlets and there is a number of excellent restaurants. Happily, the architectural scale has not been altered, with a mix of one- and two-storey buildings. Avoca, a significant newcomer, has also fitted into this village scale.

All the commercial buildings are on one side of the street facing an intact residential terrace in the early villa style. Several of the commercial outlets retain elements of the original architecture: large gate piers that opened into the stable yard, and the circular window openings that were frequently found in such buildings. Number 7a is a good example. It was in this building that the jail escapee Alfie Hinds was reputed to have run his car sales and repair business in the 1950s, while on the run from British justice.

CLOCKWISE FROM TOP LEFT THE CRESCENT BUSINESSES, 1960s; ORIGINAL CARRICKBREMNNAN POST OFFICE SIGN IN HEWETT'S SHOP; GARDAI ENJOYING CHOC ICES, MONKSTOWN POST OFFICE, VILLAGE DAY, 1989; PLAYER'S PLEASE MIRROR, MEANY'S SHOP; MEWS FOR LONGFORD TERRACE; 7A THE CRESCENT IS WHERE ALFIE HINDS RAN HIS BUSINESS; PAT DEMPSEY AT WORK IN HIS BUTCHER'S SHOP 1980s; UNDERTAKERS' DAIMLER HEADLIGHTS ON 1960s

Historic Buildings

Seapoint Martello Tower

Seapoint Martello Tower was built in 1804, one of a number of such towers along the east coast, whose purpose was to defend Ireland against an expected Napoleonic invasion. The builder was John Murray and when the building was commissioned in 1805, one sergeant and ten artillerymen were assigned to it. The invasion never occurred and the tower was never called into action. The design is based on a tower that the Royal Navy had encountered at Cape Mortella in Corsica which had been so difficult to overcome that they carefully copied the design. A small tower had enabled a small number of French to defend against a much superior British force. The Seapoint tower had a single 18 pounder cannon on top, later replaced with a 24 pounder, which could swivel a full 360 degrees. Access for the soldiers was through a doorway at first-floor level. The towers fell into disuse and, in the twentieth century, were used for a variety of purposes. Seapoint tower came into public ownership in 1901 when it was purchased by Blackrock Urban District Council. It was leased out for a variety of purposes. In 1949 a Mr Holloway sold ice-cream there, when the county council was developing the bathing facilities. For a time, Seapoint tower housed the headquarters of the Genealogical Society of Ireland, but the building proved unsuitable. In 2011, Dún Laoghaire Rathdown County Council restored the tower and placed a full-sized cannon on the roof. Tours are now organised during the summer months by the Heritage Office. The sea-bathing facilities remain very popular.

Seapoint Avenue was built to facilitate access to Seapoint Tower at the time of its construction. When the railway was being constructed, Tower Bridge was built by Dublin and Kingtown Railway Company to enable access to the tower.

Monkstown Castle

For many centuries, the history
of Monkstown revolved around
the castle. Today, what remains
of Monkstown Castle comprises a
north-facing gate-house linked to
a keep on the south by a curtain
wall. The plaster on the roof of the
entrance arch still shows the outline
of the wattles used in the original
construction. There is a small ogee
window in the gate tower facing the
interior of the castle.

Monkstown Castle would, in its
heyday, have dominated the
landscape physically as well as being
the centre of social and political
activity. It was built by the monks of
St Mary's Abbey in Dublin, probably
in the thirteenth century, to protect
their property and animals from
the attacks of the local Irish. The
first description of the castle comes
from the time of the dissolution of
the abbey in 1539. It is described
as a main dwelling surrounded

with stone walls and three towers.
In 1780, it was offered for sale
and the advertisement declared
that 'the house is magnificent,
and at the same time convenient,
equally adapted for a family of
great and moderate affluence, and
is supposed to be the second best
house in the county on the south
side of the Liffey'.

During the nineteenth century, the
castle fell into disrepair and is now
much altered in appearance. The
living quarters have disappeared,
though the outline of the pitched
roof can be seen on the side of the
south tower, and one tower has
disappeared completely. In the
1960s, the area south of the castle
was developed for housing at which
point, the stream was culverted
and the pond was filled in. It is now
known as Castle Park. The remaining
ruin is maintained by the Office of
Public Works.

TOP LEFT SEAPOINT MARTELLO TOWER,
NOW A FAVOURITE BATHING PLACE RIGHT
MONKSTOWN CASTLE BOTTOM LEFT A VIEW OF
SEAPOINT TOWER BY ALEXANDER WILLIAMS,
RHA BOTTOM RIGHT THE ROOF-TOP FURNACE
OF SEAPOINT MARTELLO TOWER USED TO HEAT
CANNON BALLS

Gone, but not Forgotten

Within living memory, a number of buildings that are intimately associated with Monkstown have disappeared. Several of these are fondly remembered by older residents.

Salthill Hotel took its name from the saltworks on the coast that operated during the eighteenth century. It replaced the earlier Coffee House which welcomed travellers through Dunleary. It was here that the celebration dinner was held when the Dublin to Kingstown railway was officially declared open in 1834. J.S. Mulvany, the architect for the railway company, designed additional rooms and, in 1865, John McCurdy redesigned the hotel in 'French chateau' style, similar to the design he employed for the Royal Marine Hotel in Dún Laoghaire. William Thackeray described it as 'a house devoted to the purpose of festivity'.

It was a luxury hotel for many years and, in the early years of the twentieth century, boasted all manner of modern amenities, such as electric light and a motor-car garage with inspection pit. The hotel prospered for a time but, by 1970, it had ceased trading and was burned down in 1972. After a decade of controversy, the site was developed with the construction of the present apartment complex.

TOP LEFT SALTHILL HOTEL LABEL **TOP RIGHT** SHANDON HOUSE **MIDDLE LEFT** SALTHILL HOTEL, 1960s **MIDDLE RIGHT** MONKSTOWN HOSPITAL, FORMERLY RATHDOWN **BOTTOM** JUGGYS WELL AND PUMPS IN THE GARDENS OF GROSVENOR TERRACE

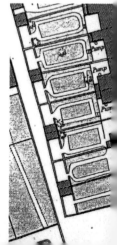

Monkstown Hospital stood where Monkstown Gate apartments now stand on Pakenham Road. The hospital was opened in 1834, with Dr William Plant as medical director, and was originally known as Rathdown Fever Hospital because it was established specifically to counteract the outbreaks of cholera. The hospital was supported by public subscription and had sixteen beds initially, which increased later to thirty-three. The hospital served the community very well until it was closed in 1987 in an early bout of rationalisation. It is still remembered with much affection by older residents.

The famed 'Juggy's Well', the principal public source of spring water for much of Kingstown and Monkstown was immediately adjacent to the hospital.

Gortleitragh and **The Slopes** have also disappeared. The former was distinguished for being the residence of the German ambassador during the Second World War and was the focus of much security interest. It had earlier been the residence of the Irish Governor-General. The Slopes was the home of the Findlater family who, as well as being Dublin's biggest wine and spirit importers, were generous benefactors of the Presbyterian Church on York Road.

The Courts of Kingstown

In describing the grand houses of Monkstown, the living conditions of the very many servants and labourers on whom these occupants depended should not be overlooked. Charles Haliday was a scathing critic of the Kingstown Town Commissioners who provided grand facilities for the wealthy and an elaborate town hall for themselves while presiding over squalid conditions endured in the many 'courts' of Kingstown. He described Baymount Court off Cumberland Street as follows:

Twenty small cottages with earthen floors, necessarily damp, as being mostly below the level of the court, which itself was unpaved and undrained, and flooded during heavy rain. To these cottages there is no rere whatsoever, nor have they the slightest provision for preserving decency and cleanliness. They have no privies, no ashpits, no receptacle for filth, which is accumulated within the doors until nightfall, when it is cast into the centre of the court, and creates an unbearable stench. There are no gas lamps or other lighting in this court.

It has no water supply, no pump, no sewer; yet it is the dwelling place of upwards of one hundred human beings, paying one shilling and six pence to two shillings and six pence per week, for single rooms twelve to fourteen feet square, in which whole families – men, women and children – eat, drink and sleep!

There were many such courts along Lower George's Street and York Road. In them, disease was rife and there were several cholera outbreaks during the nineteenth century. Haliday estimated that as many as a third of the entire population of Kingstown lived in these conditions. He also campaigned for the poor to have ready access to the sea when the railway threatened to cut them off, as a result of which a number of pedestrian bridges were constructed.

TOP BARRETT STREET, ARCHITECTURALLY PLEASING NEW HOUSING, EARLY TWENTIETH CENTURY **BOTTOM** THE COURTS OF MONKSTOWN

Monkstown then, was a place of extremes in terms of wealth and poverty. The gracious living of the wealthy occupants of fine houses and villas contrasted greatly with the poverty of the servant and labouring classes. It was the early twentieth century before the courts were swept away with the construction of public housing.

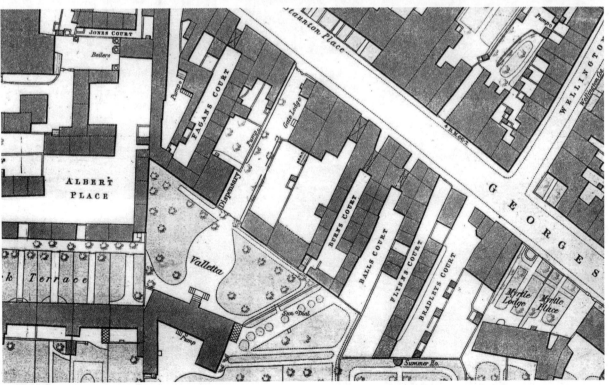

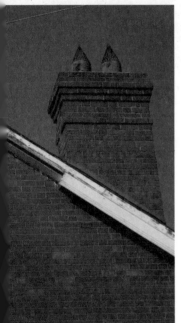

CHAPTER 3

Some Notable Monkstown Residents

During the nineteenth century, Monkstown developed as an exclusive residential area. Wealthy merchants, country landowners and professionals could now work in Dublin city and live by the sea, with all the attendant health benefits and pleasant vistas. Disease was endemic in parts of Dublin and childhood mortality was particularly high. The wealthy responded to uninhibited notices directed at 'Capitalists and Speculators' advertising land for sale along the railway line. The proximity of the harbour at Dún Laoghaire (then Kingstown) also meant that a lot of retired military, naval and colonial types settled there.

What follows are portraits of a selection of Monkstown residents of the nineteenth and early twentieth century, all of whom made their mark in some way.

The picture that emerges is of a remarkable group of individuals, among them artists and writers, scientists, architects and engineers, inventors, a few revolutionaries and, remarkably, quite a number of Christian missionaries. Two major international missionary bodies with a focus on healthcare originated in Monkstown – the Medical Missionaries of Mary and the Leprosy Mission.

Monkstown scientists, such as Grubb, Parsons, FitzGerald, Mallett and Wigham, were responsible for major innovations in their fields of endeavour and had considerable international impact. There were major scholars among them as well – Sir William Betham being an example, and remarkable humanitarians, such as Charles Haliday and William Plant. There were also a few notable fraudsters and a famous forger. All in all, a diverse and colourful lot!

MRS NORMAN MATRON, MONKSTOWN HOSPITAL, 1878–1903

Richard Brydges Beechey (1808–1895)
Artist, Naval Officer and Marine Surveyor

Passage from the east. The *Blossom* expedition also involved extensive exploration and surveying of the Pacific islands and the Californian and Chinese coasts. It was the first foreign expedition to visit California after the formation of the Mexican republic. The artworks executed by Richard Beechey during this part of the voyage have documentary as well as aesthetic value; his paintings of Inuit, and those made in California and Hawaii are now in American museums. Beechey's chart of San Francisco, published in 1833, became the authoritative guide to the bay for many years.

Beechey was invalided out of the naval service in 1831 and from 1835 his main work was on the survey of Ireland. He advanced to the rank of commander in 1846, then rear admiral and admiral (following his retirement in 1864). He was responsible for many of the charts of the north and west of Ireland, which he also illustrated with views of the coastline.

Beechey married Frideswide Maria Moore Smyth in 1840. Their youngest daughter, Frideswide Fanny Beechey was a highly accomplished chess player and publisher of chess problems.

Richard Beechey was a frequent exhibitor at the Royal Hibernian Academy (RHA), and from 1868 was submitting his paintings from

Richard Brydges Beechey was born 17 May 1808 in London, the youngest son of the noted portrait painter Sir William Beechey RA (1753–1839) and his second wife, Ann Phyllis Beechey, a noted miniaturist. The family was immersed in naval affairs and in art. Richard Brydges Beechey inherited his father's taste for painting, and shared his brothers' spirit of adventure.

Beechey entered the Royal Naval College in Greenwich in 1821 and served in the West Indies and in the Mediterranean. In March 1825, he set off with his brother Frederick William Beechey, captain of HMS *Blossom*, on a three-year voyage to the Pacific. A principal objective was to explore the Bering Strait in concert with the polar expeditions of captains Franklin and Parry, who were seeking the North-West

his home at 2 Belgrave Square. His pictures for the RHA feature mainly Irish themes, including notable seascapes of the west coast islands – Achill Island, Clare Island, Sybil Head, Slea Head, Eagle Island – as well as the entrances to the port of Limerick and Cork harbour. He painted a number of lighthouses and lightships, characteristically under rough conditions, and he portrayed yacht races, such as those of the regatta at Kingstown (Dún Laoghaire), in great detail, recording accurately the rigging and other details of the competing craft against translucent wave effects. Examples of his paintings are owned by the waterfront sailing clubs in Dún Laoghaire and the commissioners of Irish lights in Dublin. Others are at Osborne House on the Isle of Wight and the National Maritime Museum in Greenwich. He is said by Archibald in his *Dictionary of Sea Painters* to be 'the best seascape painter that the Navy ever produced'.

Beechey became an honorary member of the RHA in 1868. He also exhibited at the Royal Academy and at the British Institution. Several of these works, particularly in the period 1858–1875, were Irish seascapes. He and his wife moved to Plymouth in 1876 and he spent the last years of his life at Blenheim House on the Isle of Wight. It is interesting to note that the present owner of 2 Belgrave Square, Frank Hegarty, is also Beechey's biographer.

OPPOSITE PAGE ADMIRAL BRYDGES BEECHEY
THIS PAGE, TOP KINGSTOWN HARBOUR BY RICHARD BRYDGES BEECHEY, c.1870 **BOTTOM** 2 BELGRAVE SQUARE

Sir William Betham (1779–1853)
Genealogist and Antiquarian

Sir William Betham was born in Stradbrook in Suffolk, the eldest of fifteen children. He came to Ireland in 1805 and took up residence in a house he named after his birthplace. He was knighted in 1812. He inherited his father's interest in genealogy and became Ulster King of Arms in 1820. In this role, he was responsible for genealogical records in Ireland, a task to which he devoted himself with great dedication and energy over many years. His sister, Mathilde, was a well-known writer in her own right, and two of his sons inherited his interest in genealogy and heraldry.

He was also a prominent member of the Royal Irish Academy and published a number of works on Irish history and antiquities. He was a collector of manuscripts related to Irish history and his large collection was bought by the Royal Irish Academy in 1850. He had also sold the *Book of Dimma,* a pocket copy of the gospels in its ornate protective case or 'shrine' dating from the twelfth to fifteenth centuries, to Trinity College for £50. After his death at Stradbrook, many of his heraldic and genealogical manuscripts were bought by the British Museum and the Genealogical Office.

The Betham family was also associated with archery, and its members were prominent in Monkstown Archery Club, founded in 1846 on the site of the present Tennis Club. M.C.J. Betham, one of Sir William's sons, was described in his obituary as 'the mainstay of Monkstown Archers' Club', then one of only three in Ireland. One of Sir William's daughters was champion of Ireland on two occasions.

Sir William was very prominent in church and community affairs and was for many years churchwarden in Monkstown Church where he is commemorated in a beautiful stained-glass window. He was a member of the Board of Guardians of the Magdalen Asylum in Leeson Street founded in 1765 by Lady Arabella Denny of Lisaniskea in Blackrock, herself a great friend of John Wesley.

A bust of Sir William sits in the Genealogical Office in Dublin Castle. The family motto was: 'Per Ardua Surgam' ('Through hardship, I will overcome').

BETHAM'S GRAVE, CARRICKBRENNAN GRAVEYARD

Sir John Fox Burgoyne (1785–1874)
Soldier

Sir John Fox Burgoyne graduated as an engineer in the Royal Military Academy at Woolwich and entered the Royal Engineers. He served throughout Europe in all of Wellington's peninsular campaigns between 1809 and 1815, as well as in Egypt and Turkey. He commanded the Royal Engineers in the army of occupation in France under the Duke of Wellington after the Battle of Waterloo.

Sir John came to Ireland in 1831, when Stanley the Chief Secretary, offered him the first chairmanship of the Board of Works, a post he filled with distinction until 1846. He was responsible for discharging the very large sum of £500,000, an enormous amount at the time. In 1846, he was promoted to Major General and was also given a KGB. He held the position of Inspector General of Fortifications from 1845 to 1868 as well as serving on many commissions in England.

He received many honours, including the freedom of the City of London, and was made a baronet in 1856 and a Field Marshal in 1868. He was appointed Chairman of the Relief Commission set up in 1847 to help alleviate the effects of the Great Famine. He complained of the shocking conditions of the poor and of the practice of unscrupulous landlords in using the famine to clear tenants from their land. During this time, he used the Salthill Hotel in Monkstown as a correspondence address, though he lived nearby in Easton Lodge on Monkstown Road. Sir John was also an enthusiastic supporter of the Dublin–Kingstown railway and was a personal friend of Charles Vignoles, the engineer in charge. In recognition of his support, an engine – *The Burgoyne* – was named after him.

Sir John was also the driving force behind the creation of the Institute of Engineers of Ireland in August 1835. There was no engineering school in Ireland at the time and there was great need of technical expertise, not least in the expansion of the railway network. He was elected first president at the inaugural meeting in the Office of Public Works and, in his inaugural address, declared:

> *We are all, whether Englishmen or Irishmen, engaged in the service of Ireland and it is our duty as well as our own interest to promote prosperity to the utmost.*

Sir John died in 1874 at the age of eighty-nine.

TOP SIR JOHN FOX BURGOYNE
BOTTOM SCULPTURE IN EASTON LODGE

Colonel Sir William Cox (1777–1864)
Soldier

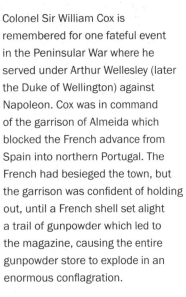

Colonel Sir William Cox is remembered for one fateful event in the Peninsular War where he served under Arthur Wellesley (later the Duke of Wellington) against Napoleon. Cox was in command of the garrison of Almeida which blocked the French advance from Spain into northern Portugal. The French had besieged the town, but the garrison was confident of holding out, until a French shell set alight a trail of gunpowder which led to the magazine, causing the entire gunpowder store to explode in an enormous conflagration.

More than 500 British and Portuguese soldiers died instantly. Cox survived and was decorated by Portugal and knighted in 1816.

He returned to Ireland and lived at 6 Longford Place and at 2 Belgrave Square. He is buried in Carrickbrennan Graveyard.

ENTRANCE TO CARRICKBRENNAN GRAVEYARD

Sir Thomas Deane (1792–1871)
Architect

Born in Cork in 1792, Sir Thomas Deane came from a family of builders and architects. He began work in his father's business at the age of fourteen and designed his first building, the Cork Commercial Buildings, at the age of nineteen. While building up a successful architecture practice, he was also prominent in public life in Cork, promoting the arts and sciences and serving as Lord Mayor on three occasions. He was knighted in 1830.

In 1860, he moved to Dublin and was elected president of the Royal Hibernian Academy in 1866. He lived at 26 Longford Terrace from 1863 to 1871.

He was the father of Thomas Newenham Deane, also an architect. Sir Thomas, his assistant Benjamin Woodward and Thomas Newenham Deane formed a partnership in 1851 which had great success in church design and in the design of public buildings throughout Ireland. Local examples include Glandore, Balnootra, the Church of Ireland Rathmichael, the Museum Building at Trinity College and the Kildare Street Club. Woodward died in 1861, but the business continued to thrive under the direction of Thomas Newenham Deane.

Sir Thomas died in Monkstown in 1871.

BALNOOTRA DESIGNED BY DEANE AND WOODWARD

Sir James Dombrain (1793–1871)
Inspector-General of Coastguards

Sir James Dombrain lived at number 8 The Hill in Monkstown, while occupying the post of Inspector-General of the Coastguard, for which he was knighted in 1843. His work required him to visit the parts of the west of Ireland that had suffered the worst effects of the Great Famine, and Sir James sometimes broke regulations to issue food to the starving population. On a visit to Killary in west Galway in 1846, he reported being 'approached by boatloads of skeletons' and he prevailed on the officer in charge of the Westport depot to distribute free meal. He also persuaded the captain of the government steamship *Rhadanthus* to take 100 tons of grain to the area. For this and other interventions, he was reprimanded for bypassing the proper procedures established by the Relief Commission. He protested that in these areas of greatest deprivation, it was impossible to establish the required Relief Committee that would raise money by private subscription and that, in any case, there was nobody who could contribute to the relief fund. To delay was to condemn the population to starvation.

As a Monkstown resident, he took a lively interest in local affairs, and was well known as a philanthropist. Like his neighbour Charles Haliday, he took a particular interest in the water supply. In 1863, the town commissioners of Kingstown were planning to improve the conditions at

TOP COASTGUARD STATION, DÚN LAOGHAIRE
BOTTOM DOMBRAIN VAULT, MOUNT JEROME

Juggy's Well, which supplied water to many small dwellings and the 'courts' where people lived in slum-like conditions. The proposal was to clean up the area surrounding the well. Dombrain's suggestion was to approach the trustees of Monkstown Hospital to allow an area to be walled off and a bucket winch erected. Another proposal was to erect an ornamental cover

over the well as was common on the continent. The town commissioners were not enthusiastic, given that the scheme to pipe water from the Vartry was to be extended to Kingstown a few years later, and the matter was dropped. In fact, Juggy's Well ran dry in the drought of June 1868, causing a major crisis. The Vartry scheme was extended to Kingstown in 1869.

George Francis FitzGerald (1851–1901)
Experimental Physicist

George Francis FitzGerald was born in 1851, the son of the Venerable Archdeacon W. FitzGerald, the rector of Monkstown Church. Having graduated from Trinity College, he became the professor of physics at the college from 1881 to 1901. He was an enthusiastic experimenter in the field of electromagnetic waves and electrolysis, and was the first to suggest a method of producing radio waves, helping to lay the basis for wireless telegraphy.

He contributed greatly to the establishment of technical education in Ireland and to the College of Technology in Kevin Street, now part of Dublin Institute of Technology, which was established in 1887 as a result of his efforts. Always interested in flight, he made an abortive attempt to fly a man-powered glider from the path outside the school of engineering in Trinity.

He is best remembered for a theory which bears his name, the Lorentz-Fitzgerald Contraction, which was the forerunner of Einstein's Theory of Relativity.

He received many honours for his work, and was an advocate of collaboration and co-operation among scientists in furthering research.

GEORGE FRANCIS FITZGERALD

Sir Howard Grubb (1844–1931)
Optical Designer and Businessman

Sir Howard Grubb was the son of Thomas Grubb who established Grubb's Optical and Mechanical Works in Rathmines in 1830. The company developed an international reputation for the quality of manufacture of precision devices, machine tools, telescopes and billiard tables.

Thomas Grubb had taken up optics as a hobby and constructed a small private observatory. His telescope came to the attention of the Rev. Thomas Romney Robinson who was director of the Armagh Observatory and it was he who first recognised Grubb's expertise and recommended him to others, as well as commissioning him himself.

Thomas Grubb completed a number of commissions for Trinity College. In 1866, the factory won the contract for a 48-inch reflector for Melbourne Observatory. Howard, who was a student of engineering in Trinity College at the time, was taken out of college and put in charge of the project. A new factory was constructed in Rathmines capable of handling the manufacture of so large a lens. When the reflector was completed two years later, it was hailed as an engineering triumph.

The firm also made refracting equipment for the observatories at Dunsink, Armagh and Glasgow, as well as astronomical telescopes that were used all over the world. Among the most notable was the 27-inch refractor for Vienna Observatory. Howard and his father also assisted the Earl of Rosse in the construction of the great telescope at Birr Castle. Howard Grubb was awarded a knighthood in 1887. He experimented with the use of photography in astronomy and built telescopes to do so. Some thirty years later, Grubb's telescopes were used to validate Einstein's Theory of Relativity. He was also involved in the development of periscopes for submarines and his Rathmines factory produced gunsights and rangefinders for the military. Grubb's Rathmines factory produced most of the periscopes for British submarines in the First World War. Before the Anglo-Irish Treaty of 1921, the British government moved the factory to St Albans in England as it was regarded as vital to British military interests.

In 1925, he joined forces with Sir Charles Parsons to found Grubb, Parsons & Co., which remained in business until 1984. Sir Howard Grubb lived at 13 Longford Terrace from 1926 until his death in 1931.

SIR HOWARD GRUBB

Charles Haliday (1789–1866)
Businessman and Philanthropist

One of the most remarkable men to have lived in nineteenth-century Monkstown was Charles Haliday. As a young man, he worked for a period in London before entering business in Dublin with his father-in-law, a timber and bank merchant. Haliday became very wealthy and was also prominent in public life, as Governor of the Bank of Ireland, Director of the Ballast Office and a Vice-President of Dublin Chamber of Commerce. He lived for a time in Fairyland in Monkstown before moving to Monkstown Park in 1843, where the Christian Brothers College now stands.

Haliday was a courageous and outspoken champion of the poor and had an early interest in providing proper sanitation and hygienic living conditions for all. He campaigned against the loss of bathing places on the coast at Seapoint and Salthill, where the railway cut across the shore, on grounds of public health more than of recreation. He was convinced that proper sanitary conditions would prevent the spread of cholera, to which the town fell victim repeatedly during the nineteenth century. He pressed the authorities to require builders to provide clean water and sewage systems for new developments. He was prominent during the cholera outbreak in 1832, when as an active member of the Mendicity Institute he notably stayed at his post, caring for the destitute. He published reports and pamphlets on the state of the poor in Kingstown which highlighted the appalling conditions in the 'courts', in which many people lived.

Haliday was a considerable scholar and wrote *A History of the Scandinavian Kingdom of Dublin*, which was published posthumously. He also dedicated himself to the collection of all possible documents and pamphlets on Ireland. This was, in fact, his principal interest, notwithstanding the energy and time he devoted to philanthropy and his business interests.

Haliday's collection grew to such an extent that when he bought Monkstown Park, he promptly demolished and rebuilt it to include a very large library. Charles Haliday died there on 14 September 1866, and the following year his widow donated his remarkable collection of 'pamphlets, tracts and papers etc. relating to Ireland' to the Royal Irish Academy, which has been the Academy's single largest donation. Haliday had requested that no headstone be placed on his grave. His wife followed his instructions but arranged that he be buried beside the boundary wall of the old Monkstown cemetery on Carrickbrennan Road, on which she placed a commemorative slab.

TOP LEFT CHRISTIAN BROTHERS COLLEGE, FORMERLY MONKSTOWN PARK RIGHT CHARLES HALIDAY, 1868, BY STEPHEN CATTERSON SMITH SENIOR (1806-72) BOTTOM COMMEMORATIVE SLAB FOR HALIDAY, CARRICKBRENNAN GRAVEYARD

Joseph Holt (1756–1826)
Insurgency Leader in the 1798 Rebellion

Joseph Holt was a prosperous farmer in Roundwood, County Wicklow, who joined the United Irishmen and espoused the ideals of the French Revolution. He was sworn to fight for the establishment of an independent Ireland and 'the unity of Catholic, Protestant and Dissenter'. He came under suspicion for treason and his house in Roundwood was burned down. This drove him into military activity with Michael Dwyer and others during the 1798 Rebellion.

He was an effective military leader and his men routed a government force at the Battle of Ballyellis, near Carnew. Even after the terrible loss at Vinegar Hill, Holt continued to lead his men against the forces of the crown. As a Protestant landowner,

he represented a particular threat to the establishment as well as being viewed with suspicion by his Catholic neighbours, particularly when it became known that his wife was interceding on his behalf with the military authorities. He and his wife were threatened with execution by the insurgents at one point.

Holt eventually surrendered. His life was spared and he was sentenced to transportation to Australia in 1799. He worked there as a bailiff and was able to buy some land of his own. In 1809, he received a free pardon and, in 1812, set out for Ireland. In the course of the journey, he was shipwrecked on the Falkland Islands but after a journey lasting sixteen months arrived back on

5 April 1814. He then lived at 72 York Road and conducted a business in Kevin Street. He later owned a pub in Kingstown. However, the businesses didn't prosper and he lived off the rents of properties he had bought. He was friendly with Sir William Betham who came into possession of his memoirs. He regretted having returned to Ireland.

After his death, his youngest son returned to Australia. The gravestone in Carrickbrennan Graveyard reads that it was erected by his son, Joshua of Sydney.

LEFT GRAVESTONE OF JOSEPH HOLT, CARRICKBRENNAN GRAVEYARD **RIGHT** PORTRAIT OF JOSEPH HOLT FROM THE HAYDEN FAMILY WEXFORD

Lady Margaret Huggins (1848–1915)
Astronomer

Lady Margaret Huggins (neé Murray) was another Monkstown resident with an interest in astronomy. Her family moved into 23 Longford Terrace when Margaret was nine years old. Her childhood interest in the stars was encouraged by her grandfather who first taught her to recognise the constellations and she began to study the heavens with her own home-made instruments.

Her interest in spectroscopy led her to the work of William Huggins, one of the premier astronomers of the day, whom she met in 1870 when he visited Dublin. The purpose of his visit was to inspect a special telescope made for him by Howard Grubb, who, in fact, introduced them.

Margaret and William were married in Monkstown in 1875, when he was fifty-one and Margaret was twenty-seven. Thus began a highly productive professional partnership that significantly advanced the science of astronomy. They pioneered the use of photography in astronomical observation, and published their research jointly. When William was created a Knight Commander of the Order of the Bath in 1897, his citation read 'for the great contributions which, with the collaboration of his gifted wife, he had made to the new science of astrophysics'. Those honoured were all men; this reference to the, by now, Lady Huggins made her the only woman even remotely mentioned in that honours list.

Together, they published the *Photographic Atlas of Representative Stellar Spectra,* but Margaret also contributed to *Observatory* magazine and to *Encyclopaedia Britannica.*

Margaret was elected to membership of the British Astronomical Association. She became an honorary member of the Royal Astronomical Society in 1892, and was admitted to fellowship on the same terms as men in 1915. She donated her scientific and artistic treasures to Wellesley Women's College in the United States. She had always taken an interest in the cause of women's education and admired the achievements of American women in the academic world.

LADY MARGARET HUGGINS

Charles Kickham (1828–1882)
Author and Patriot

Charles Kickham was born in Mullinahone, County Tipperary, into a strongly nationalist family. As a young man, he became imbued with the ideals of the *Young Ireland* movement, which diverged from the pacifist campaigning of Daniel O'Connell in favour of armed revolution. He began writing poems and stories for the Young Ireland newspaper and *The Nation*, and became friendly with the leaders William Smith O'Brien, John Dillon and James Stephens. He took a leading part in the failed 1848 Rebellion after which, having escaped capture, he lay low for a period.

On St Patrick's Day 1858, with James Stephens and others, he was present in 16 Lombard Street in Dublin, when the Irish Republican Brotherhood was founded. Kickham was appointed to the editorial board of the IRB newspaper, *The Irish People,* and became a prominent contributor. With Thomas Clark Luby and John O'Leary, Kickham was placed in charge of the IRB when Stephens went to the USA in 1864. A year later, American plans for an Irish rebellion were intercepted at Kingstown railway station, and Kickham was among those arrested in a follow-up raid on the offices of *The Irish People.* He was sentenced to fourteen years penal servitude. On his release from prison, Kickham was appointed chairman of the Supreme Council of the IRB.

2 MONTPELIER PARADE

As well as his political activities, Kickham wrote a number of novels about Irish country life, the best-known of which is Knocknagow *published in 1879. He also wrote* Slievenamon *the well-known anthem of Tipperary hurling fans.*

Charles Kickham died on 22 August 1882 at the age of fifty-four. For many years, he had been living at 2 Montpelier Place in Monkstown, which was owned by James O'Connor, a former member of the IRB and MP for Wicklow. He is buried in Mullinahone.

William Digges La Touche (1747–1803)
Diplomat and Businessman

The La Touches were a Huguenot family who fled France in the seventeenth century in search of religious freedom. The family went initially to Holland and some members ended up in Ireland following the Battle of the Boyne. The family settled in Dublin as merchants and weavers and, in time, they also established the La Touche Bank.

William Digges La Touche was a grandson of David Digues La Touche, the founder of the Irish La Touches. He was a writer, diplomat, banker and philanthropist who served the British government in the city of Basra in Persia (now Iraq) as 'resident', effectively ambassador, for almost twenty years, from 1765 to 1784. He presented his collection of valuable Persian manuscripts to Trinity College.

He acquired a reputation for humanity and generosity among the people, on one occasion paying a substantial ransom for the citizens of Zebur to rescue them from enslavement. He accumulated a considerable fortune during his time in Basra and, on his return to Ireland in 1784, became a partner in the La Touche Bank and was also a director of the Bank of Ireland. He was director and later chairman of the Grand Canal Company and La Touche Bridge in Rathmines (now Portobello Bridge) was named after him.

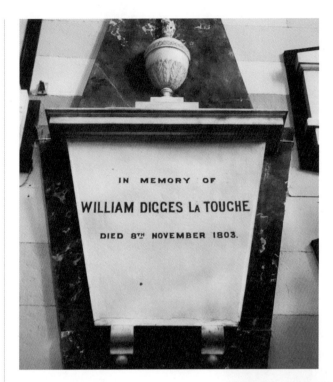

He was vehemently opposed to the Act of Union in 1800 and sought to mobilise the merchants of Dublin against it.

He was churchwarden in Monkstown at a time when the church (1785–1789) and the school (1791) were built. His wife, Grace, did a great deal of charitable work and was co-patroness of the Magdalen Asylum in Leeson Street where she worked with the founder Lady Arabella Denny.

William died suddenly from a stroke when he was about to speak at the Stock Exchange, or as one report put it: 'He died of apoplexy while visiting the stock exchange.'

TOP MEMORIAL TABLET, MONKSTOWN PARISH CHURCH **BOTTOM** LA TOUCHE BRIDGE, PORTOBELLO

Sir John Lees (1737–1811)
Secretary of the Irish Post Office

Sir John Lees was born in Scotland in 1737 and, after serving as a civilian with the army in Germany, he came to Ireland in 1767 as secretary to the viceroy. He continued as secretary to the next viceroy, Lord Harcourt, and was appointed Secretary to the Irish Post Office in 1774. This position was really a sinecure and he devoted his time to government service. In 1780, he was appointed Usher of the Black Rod in the Irish House of Parliament, a great honour at the time and, in 1781, was appointed Under Secretary to the War Department in Ireland and was created a baronet in 1804.

He lived in Blackrock House, where his holding extended as far as the site of the Martello Tower at Seapoint. In his later years, he suffered from ill health, however, we are told in a family memoir that 'he bore [his illness] with that firmness and pious resignation through life, the characteristic of his pious mind'.

> **It was some time after his death that questions were raised about the manner in which Sir John had conducted the business of the Post Office.**

He left a very considerable estate to his sons, variously reported as £100,000 and £250,000, remarkable for a man whose salary was £432 a year. In 1831, a pamphlet was published by P.C. O'Neill, a former post office clerk, in which he accused Sir John of misappropriating post office funds. O'Neill also drew attention to the appointment of John's fourth son, Edward, as joint secretary with his father at the age of eighteen. Sir John was in poor health at the time and the appointment meant that Edward was effectively the acting secretary. In 1809, Sir John was called to account and it emerged that he was in sole control of the entire business of the post office in regard to expenditure. The postmaster general took no part in the day-to-day work and exercised no oversight. O'Neill's account gave examples of misappropriation, including allowances to the Lees family for which they were not accountable. In 1807 alone, the post office lost £50,020 at a time when members of the Lees family, as well as friends, received pensions and salaries. The free post for charitable organisations was abused by another son, the Reverend Sir Harcourt Lees, author of many anti-Catholic pamphlets and letters.

Various parliamentary reports detailed extensive fraud and abuses, embezzlement of private property to 'incredible amounts', unwarrantable extravagance and waste of public money, as well as the absence of any audit of the post office between its foundation in 1774 and 1810. The private houses of officials were furnished at the state's expense, including on one occasion the repair of the Lees' piano.

In 1831, following an inquiry, Edward Lees was transferred to Edinburgh to manage the Scottish postal system and died there in 1866.

Father and son managed the Irish Post Office for two generations and accumulated a huge fortune for themselves and their families through fraud and embezzlement. Auditors were outwitted and records destroyed – they seem to have got away with it.

CLOCKWISE FROM LEFT SIR JOHN LEES; VICTORIA REGINA LETTER BOX KNAPTON ROAD; BLACKROCK HOUSE; MYRA MCGUCKIAN MAIL TO AUBURN COTTAGES

Marie Helena Martin (1892–1975)
Missionary

Marie Martin was born in Glenageary in 1892, the eldest of a family of twelve. Her father, Thomas Martin, was a partner in the firm of builders' providers, T&C Martin of D'Olier Street and North Wall. In 1900, the family moved to Greenbank in Monkstown, where the housing estate of Carrickbrennan Lawn now stands. Marie was educated in the Sacred Heart Convent in Leeson Street, in Harrogate in England and in Germany.

The outbreak of the First World War changed life for the Martin family. Marie and her sister Violet undertook training as Voluntary Aid Detachment (VAD) nurses at the Richmond Hospital and two of their brothers, Charlie and Tommy, joined the armed forces. Charlie was killed in 1915. On completion of her training, Marie was assigned to Malta where she worked among the soldiers wounded in the Gallipoli landings. She also nursed in France. She returned to Dublin in 1916 and struck up a friendship with Fr Ronayne, a new curate in Monkstown, who became her spiritual adviser.

Marie continued her charitable work and studied midwifery in Holles Street Hospital, qualifying in 1921. She responded to an appeal for lay missionaries to go to Nigeria, and quickly began to focus on health needs of the people. She had begun to form the idea of establishing a religious order of nuns devoted to medical care but, at the time, the code of Canon Law prohibited nuns from practising medicine, especially obstetrics. She returned to Ireland and then spent some time in Scotland, where she suffered a complete breakdown of health. Eventually, in 1936, the Vatican decreed that women in religious life could practise medicine, and later that year, Marie was given permission to establish a religious order. Greenbank was to be the first temporary residence of the small group who gathered around her. Marie was invited to return to Nigeria to found the congregation there, and to establish a novitiate. The congregation of the Medical Missionaries of Mary was established in Nigeria in 1937. She also established an Irish novitiate initially in Collon, County Louth, and then in Drogheda where the Lady of Lourdes Hospital was established in 1940.

Since then, the order has spread to many parts of the world. In 1963, Marie received the Florence Nightingale Medal from the International Committee of the Red Cross in recognition of her work.

LEFT GREENBANK **RIGHT** MOTHER MARIE HELENA MARTIN

Robert Mallet (1810–1881)
Seismologist and Engineer

Robert Mallet who lived for a time at 1 Grosvenor Terrace, was a pioneer in seismology. He was a civil engineer, a graduate of Trinity College and worked in his father's iron foundry in Phibsborough where he was responsible for some notable engineering projects. These included the erection of a swing bridge over the Shannon at Athlone, the Nore Viaduct, the Fastnet lighthouse and the supply of much of the ironwork for Ireland's expanding railway system. The company also cast heavy mortar launchers that were used in the Crimean War.

Several of Robert's inventions were involved with the railway: he designed a 'manumatic engine' worked by eight men which was able to carry the mail from Dublin to Kingstown in twenty minutes, and a sort of hydraulic ram for filling water tanks on the Dublin–Kingstown railway, which was of great assistance in the days of the steam engine. He also helped manufacture the railings around Trinity College, which bear the family name on the base.

Robert's principal claim to fame, however, was his work in the area of seismology, a science of which he was a founder. He conducted a series of experiments on Killiney Strand, in which he set off explosions to enable him measure the movement of shockwaves through sand and rock.

He was the first seismologist to take measurements of the epicentre of the 1857 earthquake at Naples and published a book on the subject in 1862.

He and his son also published *The Earthquake Catalogue of the British Association.*

He was awarded many distinctions: President of the Geological Society of Ireland, the Cunningham Medal of the Royal Irish Academy and the Telford Medal of the Institute of Engineers, he was also president of that body in 1866. His later years were spent in London where he died in 1881.

TOP 1 GROSVENOR TERRACE
BOTTOM MALLET FIRM RAILINGS AT COLLEGE PARK, TRINITY COLLEGE DUBLIN

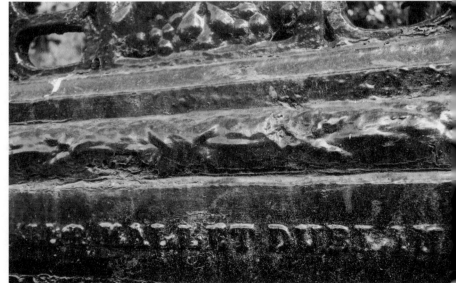

Captain John McNeil-Boyd (1812–1861)
Naval Officer

John McNeil-Boyd didn't actually live in Monkstown but is associated with it in a unique way, through his own tragic death and that of a number of companions who are buried in Carrickbrennan Graveyard. John McNeil-Boyd joined the navy at the age of thirteen and was an experienced and distinguished sailor who was regarded as a likely prospect to become a full admiral. He wrote *A Manual for Naval Cadets* which was in use in the navy until the turn of the twentieth century. As a captain, he was on board the coastguard vessel *Ajax* in Kingstown Harbour on 9 February 1861 when a violent storm struck the east coast during which many vessels in the harbour were wrecked. It wreaked havoc on shipping and caused considerable loss of life.

At about 11 o'clock in the morning, a number of vessels were seen making their way to the harbour. Three of them, the *Neptune,* the *Industry* and the *Mary,* were having great difficulty and were driven onto the rocks at the back of the east pier, at a point now marked by the Boyd memorial. Boyd summoned his men and went to the rescue of the crew of the *Neptune.* They lashed themselves together with ropes to form a human chain, to try to reach the stricken vessel from the shore. At a certain point, there was a sudden calm, followed by an enormous wave which swept the men out to sea.

All of them were drowned. In all, six of the crew of the *Neptune,* four from the *Industry* and six rescuers, including Boyd, were drowned in that single incident. It was several days before bodies were washed ashore and the funeral to Carrickbrennan Graveyard of the first four was attended by huge crowds. The funeral route was along George's Street and Monkstown Crescent and full military honours were observed. A very dramatic monument of a shattered mast marks the grave in the cemetery. Panels on the plinth list the names of the brave men who lost their lives. A grave was dug in Carrickbrennan for Boyd, but his body was not recovered for almost two weeks. He was buried in St Patrick's Cathedral in Dublin with full naval and military honours.

It is a measure of the regard in which Boyd was held that monuments were erected on the east pier in Dún Laoghaire, in St Patrick's Cathedral in Dublin, St Columb's Cathedral in Derry, Christ Church in Cheltenham (where his brother served as minister), and St Ann's Church in Portsmouth. He was posthumously awarded the RNLI Silver Medal, the Tayleur Fund Gold Medal and the Sea Gallantry Medal.

TOP SHATTERED MAST OF THE BOYD MONUMENT, CARRICKBRENNAN GRAVEYARD
BOTTOM CAPTAIN JOHN MCNEIL-BOYD

John Skipton Mulvany (1813-70)
Architect

TOP SALTHILL HOTEL **BOTTOM** KINGSTOWN STATION, DESIGNED BY JOHN SKIPTON MULVANY

John Skipton Mulvany was one of a number of prominent architects to live in Monkstown during the nineteenth century. He was the son of Thomas James Mulvany, a popular artist, and his wife Mary.

He was apprenticed to the architect William Deane Butler and completed his articles in 1833 at the age of twenty. His earliest known works were for the Dublin and Kingstown Railway and for clients associated with its directors. It has been suggested that his initial commission was due to his father's friendship with James Perry of Obelisk Park,

Blackrock, who was one of the directors of the railway company. Perry was one of a number of Quaker businessmen who saw the potential of the railway from the beginning.

Mulvany was responsible for the extension to the Salthill Hotel as well as the railway stations of Seapoint, Salthill, Kingstown and Blackrock. Kingstown Station, now a restaurant, was regarded as a particularly accomplished design, exhibiting a characteristic neo-classical style, with Ionic columns fronting a recessed portico. Throughout his career Mulvany received private

commissions from Perry and from other Quaker industrialists, including from his director colleague, James Pim of Monkstown Castle.

Mulvany lived with his parents in Booterstown until he built a house for himself at Brighton Vale in 1846, thought to be the present number 5. He probably designed the neighbouring houses over the next decade, though this is not certain. He is also believed to have designed Trafalgar Terrace and Clifton Terrace. He designed the first Royal St George Yacht Club, a modest building which was subsequently altered by Papworth. Mulvany also designed the Royal Irish Yacht Club in 1846 with its magnificent colonnaded façade. Mulvany designed railway buildings throughout Ireland: Athlone, Athenry, Galway as well as the magnificent Broadstone station in Dublin. He designed many private houses, including Mount Anville for William Dargan the railway contractor. He designed houses for other private clients throughout Ireland as well as a number of public commissions.

Mulvany married Eleanor Burke who was considerably younger than him, but the marriage was short-lived. She died of consumption at the age of twenty-five. He didn't remarry. It was said of him that he was fond of fox-hunting and cigars.

John Skipton Mulvany died in 1870 at his house in Trafalgar Terrace overlooking his first house in Brighton Vale.

Isabella (1828–1904), Charlotte (1836–1912) and Jane Pim (1840–1924)
Founders of the Leprosy Mission

Isabella, Charlotte and Jane Pim lived in Alma House on Alma Road, from which they rarely strayed during their entire lifetimes, yet they had a profound effect on the lives of millions. They were the daughters of James Pim, a wealthy Quaker who lived in Monkstown House on Monkstown Avenue.

Charlotte had a school friend by the name of Alice Grahame from Abbeyleix, who, in turn, was friendly with a young man called Wellesley Bailey. Wellesley decided to see a bit of the world before he settled down and travelled first to the Australian gold fields, then New Zealand and to New Caledonia, a group of islands in the Pacific. A second trip brought him to northern India where, after a day's teaching, he visited a leper colony where the mutilated and crippled outcasts lived in poverty. By this time, he was engaged to Alice and he wrote lengthy letters home describing his experiences, and his feelings of helplessness and frustration. Alice told Charlotte and her sisters of Wellesley's letters. Alice then went to visit Wellesley and they were wed in the cathedral in Bombay. By this time, Wellesley had begun to work among the lepers.

In September 1874, Wellesley and Alice were at home in Ireland and visited the Pim sisters at 3 Alma Road. The sisters were so affected by

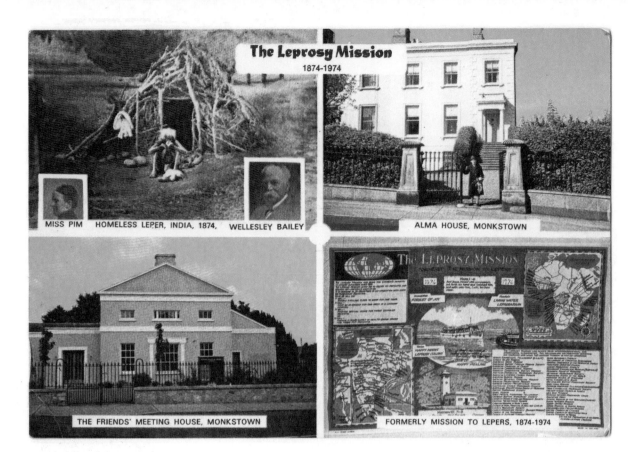

The Leprosy Mission
1874-1974

MISS PIM   HOMELESS LEPER, INDIA, 1874,   WELLESLEY BAILEY

ALMA HOUSE, MONKSTOWN

THE FRIENDS' MEETING HOUSE, MONKSTOWN

FORMERLY MISSION TO LEPERS, 1874-1974

what they heard, that Wellesley was invited to retell his story at a meeting in the Friends Meeting House (the Pim sisters were Church of Ireland, but many of the Pim family were Quakers). Charlotte undertook to raise money to support the work Wellesley had under way. Her efforts were spectacularly successful, and so began the Leprosy Mission, with its headquarters in Alma House.

Charlotte was the indefatigable honorary secretary until her death thirty-eight years later, at which point Jane, the youngest sister, took over and remained in the post until her death at the age of eighty-four in 1924. By then, the work of the Leprosy Mission had spread to many countries and had inspired many others, including Mother Teresa of Calcutta who said:

I thank God for the Leprosy Mission and its workers. It was the inspiration and dedication of the Mission to Lepers, as it then was, which gave me the example and courage to begin my work.

The headquarters of the Leprosy Mission moved from Alma House to London in 1921. By then, the small organisation that Wellesley Bailey and the Pim sisters had founded had grown from caring for forty lepers in a single facility in India, to become a large international organisation catering for thousands in many countries.

Today, the Leprosy Mission is a leading Christian organisation catering for a population of 305 million people across 200 projects in twenty-six leprosy-affected countries.

William Parsons (1800–1867)
Astronomer

William Parsons, the Third Earl of Rosse, designed and constructed a number of large telescopes to conduct astronomical research. He was born in York, England, in 1800 and attended Trinity College Dublin and Oxford University where he excelled at mathematics. The family seat was at Birr in County Offaly and he represented Offaly (which was then Queen's County) in parliament for a time. He abandoned politics however to devote his time to astronomy.

In 1845, he completed construction of *Leviathan,* the largest telescope of its day, at 72 inches (1.83 metres) to replace an earlier telescope of half its size. It was a technological triumph – all the work of construction was done by Parsons and local men on his estate. The necessary furnaces, tools and ovens were made on site, demonstrating great technical skill and practical knowledge. Many astronomers came from abroad to see and use *Leviathan,* and it contributed greatly to deepening scientific understanding of the stars and planets. Parsons claimed hundreds of new discoveries and received many honours.

> **He was made an honorary member of the Imperial Academy of St Petersburg and was Chancellor of Dublin University.**

At the time of his death in 1867, he lived at 1 Eaton Place in Monkstown. His youngest son Sir Charles Algernon Parsons invented the steam turbine engine which revolutionised marine travel, and, in 1925, he merged his company with that of Sir Howard Grubb, another Monkstown resident, to create Grubb Parsons & Co. which became a very successful manufacturer of telescopes and sights for military weapons.

RIGHT PARSONS'S TELESCOPE, BIRR CASTLE
BOTTOM LEFT 1 EATON PLACE

Richard Piggot (1835–1889)
Forger

Richard Piggot lived in 17 Vesey Place in Monkstown for many years. He came to prominence as the forger of letters which purported to come from the hand of Charles Stewart Parnell, the leader of the Irish Parliamentary Party in Westminster. The late nineteenth century was a time of great political and social tension, as the Land War raged and the Irish Parliamentary Party was pressing for Home Rule in Ireland. These letters, published in *The Times,* indicated that Parnell supported crime in pursuit of political aims and that he had specifically approved of a famous double murder of British officials Cavendish and Burke in the Phoenix Park in 1882.

Piggot was a newspaperman and had had a series of unsuccessful commercial ventures. In 1887, he concocted the idea of discrediting Parnell as a way of making money. *The Times* in London paid him £500 for the material he had produced without checking its authenticity. For a time, the publication caused great controversy and threatened Parnell's political reputation and the Home Rule project.

Naturally, Parnell sued *The Times* and the trial hinged on a spelling test: Piggot was asked to spell a number of words, including the word 'hesitancy'. He misspelled it exactly as it had been misspelled in the forged letter, *hesitency*. Piggot was exposed and Parnell was vindicated. Piggot broke down in the witness box and declared to general laughter:

'Spelling is not my strong point.'

Piggot absconded to Paris, and from there fled to Madrid. When Spanish police were alerted and sought to make an arrest, he shot himself in his hotel room, bringing a sensational end to the tale.

TOP 17 VESEY PLACE **BOTTOM** RICHARD PIGGOT FORGER

Dr William Plant (1790–1875)
Doctor

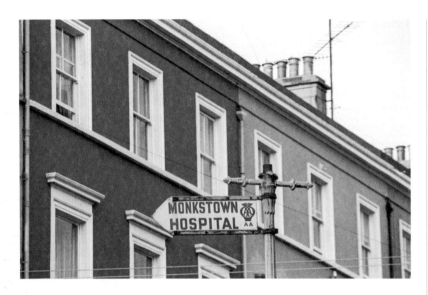

In 1822 Dr William Plant was appointed to the Rathdown Dispensary, which had a huge catchment area, stretching from Merrion to Three Rock Mountain, and from Foxrock to Killiney, and included the rapidly growing Kingstown. As the only doctor, he treated the rich and titled who were moving into the area, but the bulk of his work was 'for the relief of the sick poor', of whom large numbers lived in squalor.

He ran two branches of the Rathdown Dispensary, the Blackrock branch in Newtown Avenue and the Monkstown branch in the gate lodge of his house Plantation (now Gortmore) on Monkstown Road. The dispensary was supported by public subscription, with some assistance from the Kingstown Harbour Commissioners.

TOP OLD AA SIGN ON A GAS STANDARD
BOTTOM GORTMORE

In the twenty-three years it existed (1812–1835), a total of 28,424 patients were treated there, a huge number for the time. Given the poor sanitation and poor water supply, there was a constant threat of disease. Dr Plant's early experience as apothecary in Dr Steeven's Hospital in Dublin during the fever outbreak of 1817–1819 proved invaluable to him.

Cholera was detected in Kingstown in April 1832, and between April and July of that year, there were eighty-nine cases, of whom thirty-six died. The earlier demand for a local hospital in Monkstown was renewed and eventually a lease was taken on a site in Pakenham Road for a hospital to be called Rathdown Fever Hospital (this was later changed to Monkstown Hospital). By 1834, £500 had been collected for the establishment of the hospital and it was opened officially in 1835,

primarily for treatment of fever cases and Dr William Plant was appointed 'attending physician' assisted by a nurse and an assistant. He remained in charge for the next forty years.

This remarkable service was provided through a period of rapid population growth, through the Great Famine, and in an area which continued to suffer from poor sanitation and water supply. A second outbreak of cholera occurred in 1866. During this time, Dr Plant also conducted outpatient treatment and home visits. His own health was constantly in danger if one bears in mind that during the earlier cholera epidemic of 1833 nearly 25 per cent of doctors succumbed to the infection. He was also involved in community work, was a justice of the peace and the chairman of the Blackrock Commissioners.

Dr Plant died in 1875 at the age of eighty-five and is buried in Carrickbrennan Graveyard. Monkstown Hospital was closed in 1987 and demolished in 1989, and was replaced by the Monkstown Gate apartment buildings.

Lennox Robinson (1886–1958)
Playwright and Director of the Abbey Theatre

Lennox Robinson is best known for his association with the Abbey Theatre. He was born in Cork, where his father was a Church of Ireland rector. In 1907, he saw the Abbey Company playing Yeats' *Kathleen Ni Houlihan* and Lady Gregory's *The Rising of the Moon* and the experience made a profound impression on him. He became involved with the Abbey Company and, from 1910 until 1914, he was manager/producer at the theatre. He also spent time in London where he acted as secretary to George Bernard Shaw. In 1913, he took the Abbey players on a tour of the United States but, on account of criticism of his stewardship by Lady Gregory, he resigned. He was recruited by Sir Horace Plunkett as organising librarian for the Carnegie Trust, which was then funding local libraries all over the country, and was assigned to counties Limerick and Kerry.

In 1919, Yeats and Lady Gregory persuaded him to return to the Abbey and, in 1923, he was appointed to the board as director, a position he held until his death. He established the Abbey School of Acting in the Peacock Theatre and later, in collaboration with Dame Ninette de Valois and W.B. Yeats, he established the Abbey School of Ballet. He also wrote plays including

TOP LEFT PORTRAIT OF LENNOX ROBINSON PAINTED BY DERMOD O' BRIEN IN 1918 **TOP RIGHT** LONGFORD TERRACE **BOTTOM** DACHSHUND

The Whiteheaded Boy (1920), *Speed the Plough* (1924) and *Drama at Inish* (1933). His plays reflect a gentle and amusing view of Irish country life.

He edited and published the journals of Lady Gregory, an autobiography and the history of the Abbey Theatre. Lennox Robinson died in 1958 at 20 Longford Terrace.

He was a regular patron of Goggins accompanied by his dachshund who often had to lead him home.

The Rev. Robert Warren Stewart (1850–1895)
Missionary

Robert Warren Stewart was the son of Henry Stewart, the land agent for the Longford and De Vesci estates. The family lived successively in Longford Terrace, Monkstown House and Gortleitragh.

A Trinity graduate, Robert moved to London to study law and had a conversion experience during a church service in Richmond that led him to abandon the legal profession and become a church missionary. In preparation for his new career, he trained in the theological college of the Church Missionary Society (CMS), and was ordained. He returned to Dublin and married Louisa Smyly, daughter of the famous Mrs Smyly who established homes and schools for children in Dublin, including the Bird's Nest on York Road. in Dún Laoghaire.

Robert and Louisa embarked immediately for China, where he undertook the establishment of a theological college in Fujian province. After overcoming considerable difficulties, the college was officially opened in 1883. His objective was to set up a self-supporting native church, but because illiteracy was so widespread, he also established a three-tiered education system which would provide a steady stream of candidates for the theological college and for teacher training. He also established an industrial school.

TOP BIRD'S NEST ORPHANAGE YORK ROAD
BOTTOM REV. WARREN STEWART

He visited Ireland a number of times, and spoke at many meetings to publicise his work and raise money. He also travelled to Canada, Australia and to New Zealand with the same purpose. In all of this endeavour, Louisa was a very committed and active support.

Robert encouraged women missionaries and recruited volunteers from the women's Zenana Missionary Society to join the mission in Fujian.

Missionaries were not popular in China because they challenged traditional practices. During a period of widespread disturbance, the Stewart family was attacked by a mob. Robert and Louisa were killed, along with two of their children and four missionary women. Their other three children survived and later joined their siblings and paternal grandparents in Gortleitragh.

News of the massacre greatly increased interest in the work of the CMS in Ireland, particularly in Monkstown and a very large sum of money was raised which went to the development of the school system that the Stewarts had established. The work of the Stewarts lived on in these schools. Later, as many as five of their children were themselves to embark on missionary work in China.

John Wigham (1829–1906)
Lighthouse Engineer and Inventor

John Wigham was born to a Quaker family in Edinburgh. At the age of fifteen, he was apprenticed to his brother-in-law, Joshua Edmundson in Capel Street in Dublin. Edmundson dealt in ironmongery and ran a brass foundry, as well as developing a business in gas generation. At the age of nineteen, on the early death of his brother-in-law, John Wigham took over management of the plant, and proved to be a very successful and inventive businessman. He will always be remembered for his work in developing and improving the illumination of lighthouses, as well as for his pioneering work in electro-optical engineering.

He developed an interest in using lighting as a navigational aid at sea and invented the first successful illuminated buoy, installed on the Clyde in 1861. In 1865, the Baily lighthouse made history when the first gas-fired, high-candle-power light was put into operation. This was much superior to earlier oil lights. An improved design in 1868 was judged to be thirteen times more powerful than the most brilliant oil light then in use. John Wigham then fitted out Wicklow Head lighthouse with an intermittent gas light mechanism which enabled group flashing, the first of its kind in the world. On Rockabill Lighthouse off Skerries, he fitted a revolving lens, another significant innovation. The combination of these two inventions enabled mariners to identify the lighthouse from a distance. Wigham was also responsible for many other inventions related to marine navigation and was working on new electrical illumination systems at the time of his death.

Wigham was a civic-minded man and took an interest in community and business affairs. He became a director of the Dublin Tramway Company, was chairman of Blackrock Town Commissioners and president of the Dublin Chamber of Commerce (1894–1895). He was an advocate of temperance and twice turned down a knighthood.

He lived in 11 Trafalgar Terrace, Monkstown, for a time before moving to Albany House in 1864. He died in 1906 and is buried in the Friends burial ground at Temple Hill, Blackrock.

TOP CEILING ROSE AND LIGHT, TRAFALAGAR TERRACE **MIDDLE** QUAKER CEMETERY, TEMPLE HILL **BOTTOM** *FASTNET LIGHTHOUSE* BY CAROLE CULLEN

Image Montage Keys

1 Mrs Norman, matron, Monkstown Hospital
2 Rose thistle shamrock gate finial
3 Clifton Mews
4 Monkstown House
5 Clenched fist gate hinge, St Anne's
6 Drawers, Lane McCormack
7 Edel Quinn, aged four
8 Knox Hall
9 Neptune House
10 Brass doorknob, Longford Terrace
11 J&E Lindsay, Cobbler
12 Front entrance, St Patrick's
13 Bathroom tile, St Grellan's
14 Fr Vincent Quilter
15 Garden statue, St Anne's
16 Monkstown Parish Church (MPC)
17 Art Exhibition, Village Day, 1989
18 Doorbell, Monkstown Road
19 Dr James Gowan
20 Weighing scales
21 Lion doorknocker
22 Interior, Glandore House
23 Wisteria, Richmond Hill Villa
24 Monkstown Castle
25 Green man communion table
26 Carpet window, MPC
27 Friends' Meeting House
28 St Patrick at St Patrick's

Inside Front Cover

1	2	3	4	5	6	7	8	9	10
11	12	13	14	15	16	MONKSTOWN A VICTORIAN VILLAGE			17
18	19	20	21	22	23				24
25	26	27	28	29	30	31	32	33	34
35	36	37	38	39	40	41	42	43	44

29 Door handle, vestry room, MPC
30 Watchtower, Monkstown Park
31 Coat-hanger, Knox Hall
32 Cannon firing, Martello Tower
33 Brian O'Nolan at Clifton Avenue
34 Mosaic, Glensilva
35 Wraps, formerly Tyndall's
36 Walnut tree, Eaton Square
37 Margaret Huggins
38 Grosvenor Terrace
39 Ironwork, Eaton Place
40 Pat Dempsey, butcher
41 Richard Piggot, forger
42 De Vesci coat of arms
43 Mews, The Crescent
44 Seapoint

Pg 32–33

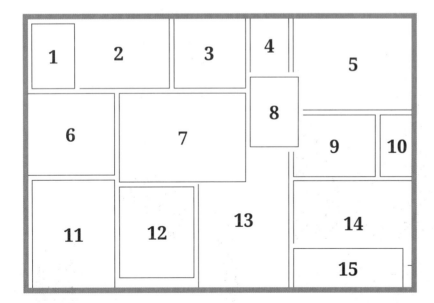

1 Gortmore, formerly Plantation
2 Tennis at The Hall School, Belgrave Square
3 Victorian footbridge over railway, Seapoint
4 Detail, Boyd Monument, Carrickbrennan Graveyard
5 Victorian footbridge, Salthill
6 Cannon firing, Martello, Seapoint
7 Converting the railway for DART, c.1983
8 Mrs Smyly in Glensilva
9 Famine tablet, Friends Meeting House
10 Edward VII pillar box
11 Old Church, Carrickbrennan Graveyard
12 William Harvey Pim
13 Train steams into boat platform Dún Laoghaire
14 St John's Mounttown Parish School
15 Lifesavers at shipwreck scene

1 Drug drawers, Lane McCormack
2 Bow fronted villas, Alma Road
3 Snowy park, Belgrave Square
4 Tile detail, Belgrave Square West
5 Corballed Vaulting, MPC
6 Decorative ironwork
7 Gable end, Belgrave Road
8 Mantelpiece detail, Longford Terrace
9 Brass doorknob, Brighton Vale
10 Venetian gothic, Glandore House
11 Fireplace, Belgrave Square West
12 Viewing window, Seapoint
13 Halliday & Co Wash Stop
14 De Vesci coat of arms
15 Berrington House, formerly Hillsborough, 1792
16 Redbricked Terrace, Belgrave Square West
17 Brickwork, Monkstown Road
18 Front door, Eaton Square

Pg 72–73

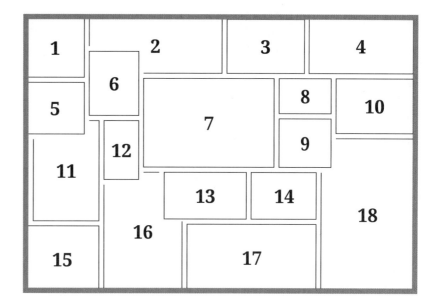

Pg 104–105

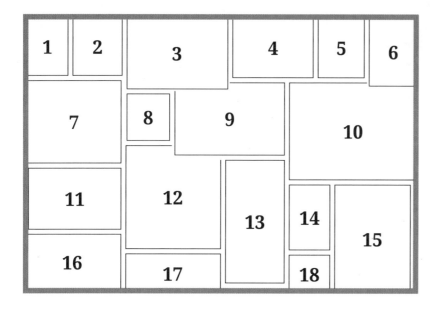

1 Gate Pier, The Slopes
2 The Rev. Billy Wynne
3 Edel Quinn in Kenya
4 Sculpture in Sir John Fox Burgoyne's garden
5 Jim Gowan on his first day at school
6 Dublin–Kingstown Railway, Salthill, 1836
7 Admiral Richard Brydges Beechey, Old Fastnet
8 Findlater's Mustard, Dublin
9 Eugene Lambert, puppeteer
10 Eileen Martin and Bart Sinnott in Capaldi's ice-cream van, 1944
11 Alex Findlater
12 Vincent Quilter at old graveyard
13 Mother Marie Martin
14 Captain McCombie, First World War & RNLI hero
15 Nurse Sarah Tait, Monkstown Parish Nurse, 1919
16 Johnny the Paperman, Belgrave Square, 1980s
17 Sailors, Kingstown, 1900s
18 First World War service medal

Image Credits

'A word about the images, firstly, the black and white images in this book were taken twenty-five years ago by Carole Cullen with the permission of parishioners and friends of Fr Vincent Quilter. New colour images, unless listed below, were taken by Carole Cullen, some of which were facilitated by property owners (prefixed by 'courtesy of'). Finally, archival images sources are given below'. **Carole Cullen.**

Page		Image Description	Source
Inside Cover	Montage	Mrs Norman Matron	Colin Scudds
		Drawers of drug labels	Veronica Cosgrove
		Edel Quinn, aged four	Concilium Legionis Mariae
		Turquoise bathroom tile, St Grellan's	Peter Pearson
		Jim Gowan, graduation	Des Gowan
		Cannon Firing , Martello Tower	Rob Goodbody
		Brian O'Nolan at Clifton Avenue	Mícheál Ó'Nualláin
		Margaret Huggins	Wellesley College Observatory, Wellesley, Massachusetts
		Pat Dempsey, Dempsey's	Courtesy of Val and Christy Moore
vii & 110		Bathing, Seapoint, 1900s	Séamus Kearns Collection
4		Monkstown Castle, Gabriel Beringer, 1766	Mossop Family
6		Dunleary Old Harbour 1760–1836 by Margaret Gowan	Des Gowan
6		Max Cheevers	Colin Scudds
7		Taylors Map, 1816	Colin Scudds
9		*Rochdale,* Shipping Disaster, Seapoint, 1807	Cormac Lowth
10		Boat train steaming into Dún Laoghaire, 1950s	Cormac Lowth
11		London Kingstown/Dún Laoghaire ticket	Cormac Lowth
11		Proposed canal and railway	Colin Scudds
17		Classroom, Monkstown Parish School with headmaster Mr Rountree	Canon Patrick Lawrence, Monkstown Parish Church
18		Christian Brothers' schoolboys, processing down Carrickbrennan Road	David Hewett
21		Domestic gas fitting, Trafalgar Terrace	Courtesy of Patricia and Michael Del Monte
22		The Blackrock and Kingstown Tramway	Blackrock College Archives
23		Royal visit, 1911	Julian Deale
24		Queen Victoria and Prince Albert at Kingstown, 1849	Cormac Lowth
27		RMS *Leinster,* Kingstown, torpedoed in 1918	Cormac Lowth
27		Convalescent from First World War at Corrig Castle	Colin Scudds
29		Gortleitragh, German Legation Second World War	Michael Goodwin
31		Ceiling cornice, Longford Terrace	Étain Murphy
32	Montage	Tennis at The Hall School 1900s	Elizabeth Sharpe-Paul
		Boat train puffing into Dún Laoghaire	Cormac Lowth
		Lifesavers at shipwreck scene	Cormac Lowth
34		Tower at St Anne's, The Hill	Étain Murphy
37		Charles Mitchel signature	Susan and Padriac Ó Brolchain
38		Ceiling Rose and Lantern	Courtesy Patricia and Michael DelMonte

40		The Hall School, Belgrave Square South	Elizabeth Sharpe-Paul
41		Norah on the steps of her home, Belgrave House	Norah Morris
48		Mounttown House, Mounttown	Kevin Strong
49		Ford Prefect, TEK advertising	Liz Neill-Watson
57		Corpus Christi Procession, St Patrick's Church	David Hewett
61		Salve	Courtesy of David and Emer Greene
61		Lane McCormack	Julian Deale
62		First Bloomsday, Goggins & Co	Maurice Keegan
62		Meany's Shop	Courtesy of Abigail Moran
62		Elton's Dairy	The Roberts Family
62		Michael (Johnnie) Lawlor, 'One Horse Power'	Colm Doherty
63		G. Byrne Newsagent, now Hewetts	Thelma and David Hewett
64		Carnegie & Co.	Ruth and Brian Carnegie
65		Gardai enjoying choc ices, Monkstown Post Office, Village Day	Courtesy Moira Brady
66		Seapoint Tower by Alexander Williams	Cormac Lowth
66		Furnace for cannon balls	Dún Laoghaire-Rathdown Co. Co.
68		Salthill Hotel, luggage label	Séamus O Connor
69		Hospital and Juggy's Well	Colin Scudds
71		The Courts of Monkstown	Colin Scudds
72	Montage	Corballed vaulted ceiling, Monkstown Parish Church	Étain Murphy
		Mantelpiece detail, Longford Terrace	Étain Murphy
		Halliday	Courtesy of Fionnuala Kelly
		Berrington House, formerly Hillsborough	Courtesy of Irwin Catherwood
76		Admiral Richard Brydges Beechey	Colin Scudds
77		Kingstown Harbour by Beechey	Cormac Lowth
85		Charles Haliday portrait by Stephen Catterson Smith Senior, 1868	© Royal Irish Academy
90		Sir John Lees	An Post
92		Greenbank	Medical Missionaries of Mary
94		Captain Boyd	Colin Scudds
94		Turret, St Anne's	Étain Murphy
98		Parson's telescope, Birr Castle	Colin Scudds
99		Richard Piggot	Julian Deale
101		Portrait of Lennox Robinson by Dermod O Brien, 1918	National Museums Northern Ireland
104	Montage	The Rev. Billy Wynne	Canon Patrick Lawrence
		Jim Gowan, first day of school	Des Gowan
		Dublin–Kingstown Railway	Séamus Kearns Collection
		Fastnet Lighthouse	Commisioners of Irish Lights
		Eugene Lambert, puppeteer	Lambert Puppet Theatre
		Capadi Icecream van and horse	Caroline Mullan
		Dublin whiskey, Alex Findlater	Alex Findlater (great-great-grand-nephew of founder)
		Sailors on leave at Kingstown	Cormac Lowth
		Captain McCombie	Tannis Pond
		Nurse Sarah Tait, Parish Nurse, 1919	The Rev. Kevin Dalton

BATHING PLACE SEAPOINT 1900s